Praise for *You Can't Drink All Day* … *the Morning*

"Whether readers are from the south side of Baw-ston or living just south of the Mississippi, Rivenbark's genuine Southern recipes and true Southern charm are sure to appeal to everyone."
—*Encore Archives*

"Many of her descriptions are not only LOL funny, they also demand reading aloud to whomever happens to be nearby."
—*Myrtle Beach Sun-News*

"Rivenbark is more than funny, she's Carolina funny."
—*The Charlotte Observer*

"Her fans can also expect to enjoy her usual tangy style of humor . . . the book is what it is, and it's all good."
—*The Fayetteville Observer*

Praise for *Belle Weather*

"Readers will laugh out loud over her commentary on status mothers and all the odd obsessions of modern life." —*Booklist*

"Think Dave Barry with a female point of view." —*USA Today*

Praise for *Stop Dressing Your Six-Year-Old Like a Skank*

"This is a hilarious read, perhaps best enjoyed while eating Krispy Kremes with a few girlfriends." —*Publishers Weekly*

"She kills in the 'Kids' and 'Southern-Style Silliness' sections, putting the fear of Mickey into anyone planning a trip to Disney World (character breakfasts must be scheduled 90 days in advance) and extolling the entertainment value of obituaries ('If there's a nickname in quotes, say Red Eye, Tip Top, or simply, Zeke, then my entire day is made')."

—*Entertainment Weekly*

Praise for *We're Just Like You, Only Prettier*

"Will give you a case of the giggles."   —New York *Daily News*

"Warm, witty, and wise, rather like reading dispatches from a friend who uses e-mail and still writes letters, in ink, on good paper."   —*St. Petersburg Times*

Praise for *Bless Your Heart, Tramp*

"Bright, witty, and warm . . . stories that make a desperate gift-giver weep glad tears of relief . . . a pleasing blend of spice, humor, and memories."   —*St. Petersburg Times*

"Celia Rivenbark has the goods and then some. She makes you laugh out loud dozens of times. Anyone who has the moxie to toss off a piece titled 'Fake Dog Testicles' will tread into the wildest stretches of comedic terrain."

—*The State* (Columbia, S.C.)

Also by Celia Rivenbark

You Can't Drink All Day If You Don't Start in the Morning

Belle Weather

Stop Dressing Your Six-Year-Old Like a Skank

We're Just Like You, Only Prettier

Bless Your Heart, Tramp

YOU DON'T
SWEAT MUCH
for a fat girl

Observations on Life from the
SHALLOW END of the POOL

Celia Rivenbark

St. Martin's Griffin

New York

www.stmartins.com

ISBN 978-0-312-61420-1

First Edition: August 2011

10 9 8 7 6 5 4 3 2 1

For my sister, Stephanie Rivenbark,
and my sisters-in-law,
Linda and Judy Whisnant

Contents

Contents

1

Taking the Class Out of Yoga

Happy, happy, joy, joy! There is staggeringly good news on the health-and-fitness front at last.

Are you sitting down? I mean, if you're like me, you're almost always sitting down, which isn't such a bad thing, as you're about to learn.

Turns out, a twelve-year-long study in Denmark has concluded that women who have skinny thighs have *twice* the risk for heart disease as us normal women.

Can I get a "Nah, nah, nah, *nah,* nah," my fluffy sisteren?

In your *face,* you supermodels with your spaghetti stems. Somebody please pass the pork fat and let me get on with the very serious business of avoiding a heart attack. I am all about being heart-healthy.

The study followed twenty-eight hundred Denmarkese

(yeah, I know, but the real name makes me hawngry) and discovered that the portion of the population with thighs smaller than 23.6 inches in circumference had twice the risk of heart disease.

OK, to be honest, I thought that 23.6 inches sounded like a *lot* of inches when I first read that. I mean, that's like almost two feet of inches if my math memory is correct. So I got out the old tape measure and y'all guess what?

My thighs, which are actually kind of thighnormous, are exactly 23.5 inches. Too much information? Suckit, I'm fit by Denmarkanian standards!

The study doesn't explain why thicker thighs make a healthier heart but who the hell cares and, yes, I want fries with that Communion wafer.

There's some speculation that it's because thinner people (hereinafter referred to as "the damned") have less muscle mass to "initiate the metabolic breakdown of lipids and glucose." I mean that's the first thing I thought when I read about it. Sorta. If you remove the part about metabolic breakdown of lipids and glucose.

This news came with caveats, of course. Caveat is a Latin word which means "dead person" or "funny neckerchief," I forget which. Anyway, the big caveat is that people who have thighs quite a bit bigger than the delightful and healthful 23.6 inches in circumference (in other words, anyone who has ever eaten a turkey leg at Disney World and wondered why they have to be so damn small) aren't healthier by nature. They have gone and gotten themselves a bad case of an "overhealthy heart" I guess.

Scientifically speaking, the study finds that a woman who is barely over five feet tall and weighs 135 pounds is half as likely to have heart disease as, say, Heidi Klum.

Now before all you supermodels get your Versaces in a wad and accuse me of wanting you to have heart problems, let me hasten to say that nothing could be further from the truth.

Scurvy maybe, pellagra possibly, but not heart trouble. It also should be noted that Denmark is frequently the winner in the annual poll of the "World's Happiest Countries." Small wonder. I'd be happy, too, if I lived in a country where big thighs were considered healthy and desirable.

This breaking news from Denmark came out just about the same time as a *Time* magazine cover story on "The Myth of Exercise" in which a very learned scholar wrote that, while it's good for you, exercise won't make you lose weight. In fact—and this part cracks me up—exercise can actually lead to weight *gain* because of the notion that you're entitled to wolf down a platter of nachos the size of a hubcap at On the Border after a half hour workout on the Spawn of Satan, I mean, elliptical machine.

Your chickens have come home to roost, you diet-obsessed hand-wringers. And I want mine fried with a side of tater salad, extra mayo for my heart, natch.

Ever since I read about the study of the proud Denmarki

people, and the *Time* exercise story, I've been thinking about cutting out my weekly yoga at the art museum, but I like it too much. Except for the parts where the middle-school classes taking tours past the Mary Cassatts and so forth point and laugh at us when our asses are in the air for Downward-Facing Hag or whatever you should call a roomful of mostly middle-aged but undeniably enlightened womenfolk in loose clothes.

What if all this yoga makes my thighs get smaller? Still, I'd hate to give it up because yoga really does give me a certain peace and clarity of spirit.

OK, I made that up. It just feels good to be somewhere for a whole hour without anybody being able to find me and ask me to do some shit for them.

I'm fairly certain that's why it was invented many decades ago by Yogi Berra, a famous baseball player who was excellent at avoiding real work.

I never saw myself as a yoga-type person but then I read *Eat, Pray, Love*, whose author, the glowy, flowy Elizabeth Gilbert, described how her deep and intense voyage of self-discovery, which included dumping her perfectly nice husband and visiting several different continents, led her to realize that she could eat nine pizzas at one sitting in Italy and still feel good about it if she was headed to India to do some yoga.

I think there was a little more to the book than that, but that was my favorite part.

Yoga just sounds so cool. Our teacher, a young woman

fairly bursting with good health, meets us where we are, so to speak.

"You can rest when you need to," she said on the first day of class, seeming to look at me for a long time—perhaps because I was the only one who had never had so much as a smidgen of yoga before. She knew this because I announced it, repeatedly, so she'd set the bar pretty low.

I was delighted that she understood, and so I did rest. For an hour. Just lay there on the purple yoga mat my friend Christy Kramer got on a yard sale for fitty cent and loaned me when I told her I didn't want to invest a whole lot of money into this yoga stuff until I was sure I'd like it.

Sure, some of the other women looked puzzled when I lay down and stayed down, but what can I tell you? It was the first time in for-freakin'-ever that I'd had some me-time, phone off, panties granny, and it felt wonderful.

Laying there while the others practiced some serious deep breathing and challenging poses like Old Pussy in the Sky or some such, I understood why everybody loves yoga. I went to sleep.

And was awakened an hour later by the instructor gently kneading my thigh. My perfect, enormous thigh.

"Uhhh, trying to sleep here," I mumbled, but she just smiled one of those real peaceful yoga-induced smiles. "We want to keep the muscles as relaxed as possible."

Was she high? If I was any more relaxed, I'd be in an urn on somebody's mantle. I was deliciously relaxed and now understood why people who take naps in the middle of the day always feel so refreshed. At this rate, I'd be one of those irritating people who has a license plate holder that reads: MY OTHER CAR IS A YOGA MAT! OK, maybe not.

After that, she announced that we would take some deep breaths and thank our sun gods or something like that. It involved putting your hands in front of you and making a praying gesture for about two seconds, which, let me tell you, my muscles paid for the next day! I practically couldn't get outta bed!

Yoga is going to be a much better fit for me than, say, Pilates, which, because I was raised Southern Baptist, I mispronounced for a really long time until my unchurched, heathen friend told me it had nothing to do with Pontius Pilate.

"It's pronounced puh-*lot*-eez," she said with clear irritation. She is one of those snooty types who talks a lot about how all the hypocrites are in church and she believes that God is everywhere around her.

Not meaning to be cruel, I hope for His sake this wasn't true the day she seriously cut one in yoga class.

That's the dirty little secret about yoga. All the pooting that goes on. Sure, you can try to sneak it out in low gear, so to speak, but everybody still knows. So while you're in your Loving Warrior Stance when you should be breathing deeply and feeling the life force gum up your chakras or whatever, you're just worried to death that the whole class is going to hear you fart out loud.

I'm not sure how Elizabeth Gilbert dealt with that because there's no way you could eat nine pizzas for lunch and then go to yoga, even if it was a few days later. You'd still be floating up in the air like that idiot balloon boy.

I think I'll keep doing yoga for a while, staying away from the new "yogilates" class I've heard about which combines yoga and Pilates with a foamy cappuccino concoction from the sound of it. After all, even though I'm not making real progress in the meditative closing moments when I'm supposed to be open to the universe and, instead, routinely make my grocery list in my head and worry about how unfair it is for me to need gum grafts at the same exact time that my kid needs orthodontia and where the hell is all that money going to come from. . . .

The instructor says that all of this openness to the will of the universe takes time. One doesn't just leap into meditation. It can takes years of practice, even Elizabeth Gilbert said that. But, in the meantime, while I'm waiting for that to kick in, I'll continue to eat pizza.

Just for the sake of my heart, you know.

2

When Underwear Jokes Bomb, the Terrorists Win

Does it mean I have to turn in my liberal card if I admit that I actually *like* the notion of profiling terrorists at the airport?

Here's the thing. I want to be against profiling, really I do, but I just can't get past the fact that as much as I want to be fair and logical and open-minded, all that high-minded crap is overshadowed by my fervent desire for my ass not to be blown out of the sky.

So, after much soul searching (OK, actually not that much; I've taken longer to toast a Pop Tart if we're being frank here), I have decided that the TSA should go for it.

TSA, for those of you who don't follow the news like I do (while cooking dinner, drinking box wine, and screaming at my kid every ten seconds to finish her damn science project), stands for the Transportation Something Administration. These are the folks who are charged with keeping us safe in the sky and stuff.

Bottom line: I've decided the TSA should profile suspicious characters. Hell, even nonsuspicious ones. If someone acts just a little odd (furtive glances, shifty eyes, annoying under-breath chanting of "death to American pig scum," etc.), then the TSA should profile the hell out of them. I don't care if they just have a *hairstyle* you don't like, go for it, TSA!

Ever since that creep flew into Detroit with junk in his trunk, planning to blow everyone to bits on Christmas day, I've changed my whole way of thinking about profiling.

TSA, if you see somebody suspicious, I don't care if you strip search 'em and force 'em to sit for hours in a detention room the size of a Triscuit. I repeat: I don't want my ass blown out of the sky. Or yours, either. I'm bighearted that way.

But what of the trampling of individual rights, you ask? Hey, like Gandhi or somebody said, you can't make an omelet without breaking a few eggs. And if those eggs happen to be stamped u.s. CONSTITUTION, well, that was written way before air travel so it's not terribly relevant.

Face it: The founding fathers might have even embraced some profiling but those were simpler times. When teeth were made out of oak trees and everybody kept poop in a pot beneath their bed. Frankly, it was all a little weird.

The TSA needs to step it up, though, and I'll tell you why.

If you'll recall, the terrorist dude paid cash, bought a one-way ticket, and didn't have any luggage.

These are things that most security officials and, well, people who breathe in and out many times in the course of a day, would aptly call "red flags." Wouldn't it have been positively Smurfy if someone had noticed the terrorist bought a one-way ticket, paid for it with cash, and didn't have any luggage? Wheel, meet asleep person.

The TSA needs an overhaul, and this should worry all of us. While crazy people with no luggage and exploding underwear board with abandon, my eighty-nine-year-old friend—think classic Rockwellian grandpa wearing a cute ball cap covered in collectible battleship pins—was frisked like a whore in church (OK, wrong metaphor but you get the idea) while trying to get to 'Bama for his grandson's wedding. What up with that?

I was flying on bidness a few months ago and standing right behind a female soldier wearing full-camouflage uniform as we waited to go through the metal detector. As she stepped through, the alarm went off and a TSA worker had to wand her. It happened four or five more times until I finally pointed out that she was wearing a banana clip in her hair that was probably causing the ruckus. She removed it, the alarm stopped beeping, and no fewer than three TSA workers grinned happily at me and said, "Hey, thanks!"

I hate to overstate the obvious but when y'all are depending on me for airport security, there is a huge problem. I just happen to know about banana clips. (And I'm wondering: Where did she find that thing, since I haven't seen one of those since *Full House*?)

I know what you and the other members of my yoga class are thinking: But, Sistermaiden (that's my new yoga name), you must realize that profiling is a very flawed system of protection.

True that. After all, terrorists could easily switch gears and recruit blond, blue-eyed sympathizers to put explosives in their underpants and fly all over the world. It's not that hard to disguise yourself. Remember how Philip Kiriakis got an entire face transplant on *Days of Our Lives* a few seasons ago? I can't believe terrorists didn't see that story arc and learn a little something from it. And who among us can honestly remember what Carrot Top used to look like? Or poor Mickey Rourke, brilliant in *The Wrestler* but still kinda goofy, what with that Chihuahua on his arm at the awards shows and all.

So, yes, I guess it's possible that as soon as you start profiling for only dudes rockin' the smelly/swarthy vibe with noticeable bulges in their bottoms, the terrorists will just switch gears.

Hey, I know that the overwhelming majority of Muslims in this world are kind, decent folk who only want to work hard, worship peacefully, and raise happy, healthy families. Everybody knows that. But look at it this way: You're walking down the street and you see a tiger on one side and a dog on the other. OK, it can be Mickey Rourke's Chihuahua for the sake of illustration. Which side do you want to walk on?

I'll give you a hint: It ain't the tiger's.

One of the worst things to come out of all this was the inevitable onslaught of bomb-in-underwear jokes, which should only be attempted by truly funny people. Bomb jokes aren't for amateurs. Consider the fact that a German family lost out on their whole vacation after the dingbat daddy, all boisterous in anticipation of a holiday with his wife and daughter, cracked wise at the Stuttgart airport.

"Hey! I got explosives in my underwear!" he said. While everyone shifted uncomfortably in line, don't you know his wife was mortified and his daughter was rolling her eyes and texting her friends about how lame her dad was? It reminded me of the time—OK, the many times—duh-hubby, the Princess, and I have vacationed only to have Duh be the one in the tour group at the antebellum home/space museum/petting zoo to ask questions of the guide. While the Princess and I visibly cringe, Duh will pepper the guide with all sorts of inane questions. ("Yes, but who was the *third* man on the moon? We'll wait while you look that up.")

German guy wasn't so much harmful as clueless of correct comic timing. You can't, just days after the plane incident, say stuff like, "Yep, I'm a *little bit* worried about servicing all those virgins once I get where I'm going but, Allah be praised, I'm sure there will be a way. Hahahahahaha! Did I mention that my underpants are explosive?"

This is a great example of why humor should only be attempted by professionals. This guy, perhaps overly giddy at the notion of a much-needed weeklong vacay away from the sausage factory or making my next car, went too far. And he has the unpleasant body cavity search by Lars to prove it.

Still, he gets points for trying to wring something funny out of current events, even when they're decidedly unfunny. Any story involving the word "underpants" has the potential for comic gold. Any story. Trust me. This is what we in the Professional Humor Business call "a sure thing."

There are just some news headlines that seem ripe for fun-making. Take the time Obama invited the Cambridge cop and the professor to the White House for a beer in hopes that they could make up. While others thought this was a unique approach to opening a much-needed dialogue about race relations and, yes, profiling, my first thought was: "Oh, hells yes! I'm gonna ask Obama to help me patch things up with the carpool bitch who *always* gets out of her car and disappears to chat while we all have to drive around her stupid van." If the leader of the free world has time for this sort of thing, I am so in!

The other thing about the German would-be jokester is that he didn't understand when to quit. You can't keep telling the same joke over and over. Unless you're Larry the Cable Guy. No, I was right the first time. You really can't.

Dave Barry, a little-known comic who, I believe, lives on a bed of plantain peels in a Miami alley, once noted that humor has to be a *series* of punch lines. You can't just have one joke in your arsenal. That said, you also should be careful to always leave 'em wanting more. Jon Stewart? Yes, please. Carlos Mencia? Not so much.

The problem with our German friend is that his timing was off. Way off. It's the same reason it's OK now to joke about Michael Jackson but right after he sailed away on a puffy cloud of injectibles? No flippin' way. Only now is it acceptable to joke about those wacky Jacksons. And while I'm glad the chirren have found a stable home with Michael's mom, I have to wonder if it wouldn't be better if they were in the care of someone a little younger—say, Methuselah.

The important thing to remember is that in humor, timing is everything. The German guy could've tried out his best Michael Jackson material instead of the underwear-bomb joking and nothing would've happened except the Germans, who love 'em some *Thriller*, might've been pissed.

All of these are weighty matters that are best left to the deep thinkers among us. Yeah, that's right: Dane Cook.

3

Movie To-Do List: Cook Like Julia, Adopt Really Big Kid

I went to see *The Blind Side* with duh-hubby and the Princess a while back. For those of you who haven't seen it, *Blind Side* is a fuzzy-wuzzy inducing movie in which Sandra Bullock plays a tough-talkin' Southern belle married to a Taco Bell mogul. One day, she discovers a homeless high school boy walking alone in the freezing rain and immediately stuffs him into her fancy imported car and takes him to her house, where he will spend the next few weeks sleeping beneath an Yves Delorme comforter on her couch. Which strikes me as weird, since her crib looks like it would have at least a dozen spare bedrooms. Let's just say that gorditas have been very, very good to this family. She works a little, too, as all good tough-talkin' Southern belles do, and naturally it's as an interior decorator. This makes it possible for the movie to include a few shrieking phone calls to some off-camera and impeccably gay assistant to show that, yes, she is quite tough-talkin'. It's easy to see how she'd fall for her husband. When I think Taco Bell, I think interior design, don't you? Aye Chihuahua!

No matter. She is the classic Southern woman who will move mountains for those she loves, including and especially her new black son. She spends the crucial first few weeks together with him teaching him how to coordinate his Abercrombie with his Fitch. Along the way, the kid becomes a football star at the fancy private high school her kids attend, which isn't a real surprise because this kid is frikkin' *huge*.

All I can think is thank God Almighty that kid's birth mama supposedly smoked lots of crack or he would've come out weighing, like, forty pounds when he was born.

The movie was pretty good but I had a hard time concentrating because there was another bright screen just a Twizzler's breath away. A woman I'll call Turdette was sitting beside me and spent the whole movie compulsively texting on her Dingleberry, which had a screen bright enough to land a jumbo jet on a rainy runway.

It was so annoying that I almost missed the best scene, where Sandra Bullock chews up her bigoted lunch buddies at the club and spits 'em out like Sanka at Starbucks.

Even Turdette paused momentarily from her texting to watch, but then she went right back to it.

I shouldn't be surprised. The movie theater is the last bastion of lawlessness in polite society.

Where else can you just toss your used food and drinks on the floor? I mean besides the opera, of course.

Movie theaters have always had a slightly seedy vibe and not just because the back row is always reserved for blow jobs. Which I tried to explain to my mother as she headed up the steps toward the top row when I took her to see something forgettable starring Catherine Zeta-Jones, who, she made a point of saying, "looks like she'd be the kind of daughter who would treat her mother very nicely."

"You can't sit there! That's where the kids sit. It'll be noisy and, uh, gross."

"I bet Catherine Zeta-Jones would let her mother sit anywhere she'd like," she huffed.

"But this is the illicit sex row! Everybody knows that. Children have been conceived back here. Remember that girl in the Princess's home-ec class? The one who named her son Avatar? You think that was just a coincidence?"

"You don't know what you're talking about," she snapped. "I've got a bad back. I have to stand up every ten minutes. Do you really want me to do that in the middle of the theater?"

Point taken. We sat in the back row and I breathed a huge sigh of relief when a bunch of older folk showed up and filled in the rest of the row. Throughout the movie, it was like everyone had little national anthems playing in their heads as they periodically popped out of their seats and just stood there for a minute or two cracking and stretching before sitting back down.

From our perch on high, I could see all sorts of moviegoing malfeasance. For starters, there were the latecomers. These tardy assholes like to come in and ask you to scoot down so they can take an aisle seat.

What they don't understand is that dues have been paid for that aisle seat. Until you've suffered through seventeen minutes of movie trivia ("Sandra Bullock was born in Arlington, Virginia!"), all I've got to say is talk to the imitation-butter-soaked hand.

Another violation? Using your coats and assorted shit-wear like crime scene tape, to rope off a bunch of seats just so your trifling friends will have somewhere to sit when they stumble in late.

And then there's the creepy theater-etiquette violation: If the theater is practically empty (think any Steven Seagal comedy), make sure not to sit close to the only other person there. That's just plain pervy.

Without a doubt, the worst movie behavior isn't bright screens, pervs, saved seats, or latecomers who lean over to ask, stupidly, "Is this seat taken?" spilling half their popcorn into your lap or (back row only) your girlfriend's head.

Just because you've seen a movie once or twice, this doesn't entitle you to spoil it for the rest of us. Don't say, "You know he ain't coming back alive, right?" when Diane Lane watches her beloved Richard Gere speed off in his fancy-doctor car to save sick orphans.

Years ago, I was watching *Pay It Forward* when the clod behind me coarse-whispered to her friend, "This one has a sad ending." The friend tried to shush her but it didn't help. "I mean this is the saddest ending I've ever seen. You're not gonna believe it."

The friend said, "Shhhh!" again but the coarse whisperer was unstoppable. "Well, I'd just better tell you, don't get too attached to that little boy with the eyes that remind you of Hummel figurines 'cause, well, he's gonna get dead!"

Overall, I love going to the movies, although there are some I wish I'd just waited to rent instead. Like *Marley & Me*. It's another fuzzy-wuzzie inducer based on a book that a newspaper columnist wrote about his mischievous lab dog.

And by "mischievous" I mean shithead.

As my fellow moviegoers stumbled out sobbing into their tissues and remembering their own long-gone pooches, I asked Duh if I was the only one in the whole damn theater who thought Marley needed to die a lot sooner.

When the "rascally" Marley tripped the couple's toddler, who happened to be human and still possessing a soft spot on his little noggin, that would've done it for me.

"That kid could've had a hematoma!" I said.

"You don't understand dogs," Duh sniffled, pausing to look at a faded picture in his wallet of his childhood dog, Tyrone, who died twenty-seven years ago, I kid you not.

"Don't you get it? Dogs are perfect creatures because they love you unconditionally," he said. "They have no expectations and they make no demands."

"Well that's just messed up," I said.

What good is love if you can't extract something fabulous in exchange for it? Well? I'm waiting here.

A red-nosed theatergoer who overheard all this gave me the stinkeye on the way out. What can I tell you? I'm a shallow creature who craves order and calm. If I walked into my living room and discovered my "lovable" dog leaping about in a snow-storm of couch stuffing, I'd have to be sedated. Seriously.

The book which *Marley & Me* is based on sold millions and made John Grogan very rich indeed. Maybe now he can afford a cat. His newspaper career was steady but unspectacular until he started writing columns about his dog's latest misbehaviors. Having been a newspaper columnist for a couple of decades, I can tell y'all that writing about your pets is what we in the bidness call "pulling one out of your ass." It's right up there with the "from the mailbag" desperation column. These columns usually, in journalistic terms, reek.

But in Grogan's case it clicked. Which means that my next book will be a collection of heartwarming stories about the antics of my three cats. Look. It's not like old, dying professors named Morrie are growing on trees, right? Between columnist Mitch Albom's Morrie and Grogan's damn dog, I need to read the handwriting on the Whiskas.

If that doesn't work out, I can always write a book like

Blind Side. I will cruise the highways and byways looking for an exceedingly large and innately talented young man whom I can befriend in hopes of selling my screenplay. (Plus, this will get those exchange student nags off my back. Why would I want to take in some kid from another country who doesn't even *understand* football?)

Duh thinks this is all a tad ridiculous. But until he becomes a Taco Bell mogul (God, I love that phrase), I'm not paying a lot of attention to what he has to say.

"You start coming home with sacks full of pillowy cheesy goodness and then we'll talk," I huffed.

Despite our movie friction, we trudged out to catch *Julie & Julia*, about spunky New York blogger Julie Powell who cooked all 534 recipes in Julia Child's cookbook in just one year.

What can I tell you? I had myself a good old-fashioned epiphany. The next day, I sat down the fam and made my announcement.

"Don't try to stop me," I said, shoving my own copy of Ms. Child's ginormous *Mastering the Art of French Cooking* toward Duh with my foot because it is simply too heavy to lift.

"I know it sounds crazy but I'm going to cook one recipe from this book at least once a year."

There. I said it. No applause, please.

"Big deal," said the Princess, who stomped out of the kitchen to return to her full time-job: staring at the life-size poster of Robert Pattinson in her room. Oh, wait. That's my room. Well. I like to support the arts whenever I can.

"Once a *year*," mused Duh as he constructed the only thing he knows how to make: vanilla wafers stuffed with peanut butter. "But in the movie, she makes something every single day. That was kinda the whole point, wasn't it?"

"Well, I believe we established that she was spunky, which I am not. Go ahead: Pick out any dish you like from this book and I will make it. Some day. Within the next year."

Naturally Duh went straight to some amazing looking multilayered torte thingy dripping with chocolate ganache.

I love the pictures in this cookbook more than anything. I love pictures of food in general. It's why I'm curiously bitter when eating at fancy gourmet restaurants, because they almost never have pictures of food on the menu. Except Olive Garden, of course.

Truly, the only fault I could find with *Julie & Julia* was a definite shortage of food porn. I love a movie like *Like Water for Chocolate*, where there's food in every single scene. The camera did linger lovingly over Child's classic beef burgundy for a few extra blissful seconds, but I craved more naked butter shots.

Julie & Julia went a long way toward restoring my food equilibrium after watching *Food Inc.*, a nauseatingly well-done documentary about where hamburger comes from. For months, I had only been able to buy organic chickens, tough old birds who dropped dead in their tracks from a life well lived. The kind of chicken that was given a little bonnet and shawl to wear at night to ward off a chill. The kind of chicken that would stand up in the last row of the theater every so often just to stretch.

So, yes, the movies have a huge effect on me. I started going to the local farmers' market but felt like an outsider because I (a) shave my pits and (b) think patchouli smells like ass.

No matter. I'm learning. And in the meantime, there's that torte to make. Sometime in the next fifty-one weeks.

4

Kiosk Bee-otch Makes Mall Trip Treacherous

A skinny woman in a white coat jumped in front of me at the mall.

"Ess-cooz-uh me, ma'am. Do you wor-ray about the moisture in your skin?"

Her tone was shrill and a tad desperate. Apparently it had been a long day. Her Bumpit was listing to one side as though she was hiding a chocolate muffin in her hair for later.

She pointed a pump dispenser of lotion at my face and, without looking down, reached for my hand.

What the hell?

"Give me your hand!" she fairly shrieked. "I will make it beautiful."

Unless she was planning on presenting me with the diamond eternity band that I've been hinting to Duh about for the better part of twelve birthdays, this conversation was officially over.

"No thanks," I muttered. I tried to walk away, but damned if she didn't lurch back in front of me. The desperation reminded me of those movies where the pimp is secretly lurking across the street to make sure his hos are really giving it their all.

I looked around but didn't see anyone resembling a pimp. Just a fat guy eating a fried hot dog wrapped in pretzel dough and rocking in a rocking chair.

One thing I love about a mall is that they don't even bother to pretend. This is not a place of restraint and fitness. This is a place where you can eat at seventy-five places within fifty feet, then collapse into a chair and rock your fat ass right into sleepyland. It's a little like I imagine heaven, if you must know.

"I don't want any of that stuff," I told her. She looked pissed but quickly regrouped, smoothed her Bumpit and scurried away to offer to make beautiful someone else. Pretzel-dog guy wiped some mustard off his chin in his sleep. Nah, he was no lotion pimp.

As I journeyed deeper into the impacted bowels of the mall's kiosk court, a man in a shiny shirt and tight black pants gave me his best smile-by-Lumineers.

"Madam, if I may ask, wouldn't you like to have the shiny hairs?"

Ooooh, the shiny hairs.

He was holding some sort of flatiron gizmo in one hand and tapping it on the palm of the other hand. The gesture reminded me of a cop with a nightstick. Except instead of wanting to subdue me with force, he wanted to give me the shiny hairs.

"No, thanks," I said with way more courtesy than I felt. He trotted along behind me.

"Madam, I just want to show you something *amazing!*"

Something told me it wasn't his Mensa scores.

There were other offers as I continued to wade through kiosk hell.

"Lady! A massage today! Very relaxing, make you a new woman. . . ." There was even someone who wanted to throw me into a recliner and thread my eyebrows. I have no idea what the hell that is but I'm pretty sure it's not something you want to do in public. What's next? Quickie Brazilians by the Dippin' Dots?

Mom: "Junior, you and Sister go get you some 'nanner ice cream. Mama's gone be right here gettin' her cootch waxed. What do you mean you've lost your appetite?"

A woman dressed in a long gingham apron and wearing fake wire-rim glasses hollered to no one in particular: "Glazed pecans, better'n your granny made!"

OK, first, my granny never made glazed pecans. She didn't make much of anything except the world's best bread pudding. I could've happily lived off that bread pudding and nothing else, but my sister and I both used to squirm when she would offer to cook supper for us. Invariably, she'd burn a couple of quarter-inch thick T-bones, then cover them with a bitter-tasting snowstorm of some ghastly salt substitute.

Glazed pecans? Not so much.

A few steps farther away from Pepperidge Weirdo I was confronted by a greasy teenage boy who grinned demonically while tossing a toy glider dangerously close to my head. It boomeranged back to him just in time. He looked at me and grinned loopily. Hmmmm. Looks like somebody took time out to visit the Ecstasy kiosk.

I was still pondering how close I'd come to getting a toy plane up my nostril when a woman in her twenties sprang at me like a cheetah.

"Can I see your nails, miss?"

I frowned and walked past her but she was quick and I nearly tripped over her. I was now officially pissed off.

"You no want bee-you-tee-full nails?" she asked with a little fake sad look.

"Nope," I said. "And no soft hands, pecan cones, eye-putting-out toy planes, shiny hairs, or public backrubs, either."

But there was one thing I realized I wanted very much. A fried hot dog wrapped in a pretzel. The grease would be good for my cuticles.

There was a long line at the pretzel shop, so I had time to consider that a smoothie would be a lot healthier. Besides, did I really want to end up in a rocking chair coated in mustard and suspected of being a pimp? A smoothie it would be.

But nothing is easy these days, my hons.

Me: "I'll have a strawberry smoothie, please. Small is fine."

Clerk: "Certainly. Do you have a rewards card with us?"

Me: "Huh? Uh, no. I don't. Sorry."

Clerk: (brightening): "Oh, don't worry! You can get one today. You can save 5 percent with every purchase if you just fill out this (sounds of papers folding out and onto the floor) membership application. The annual fee is only $20!"

While I snorted at the notion that my "membership" might be passed over by some committee in a plush board room somewhere (it's not exactly an exclusive "club" when the application is handed to you with banana goo on it, now is it?), the clerk was patient.

Me: "So, if I give you $20 now, I'll save, let's see . . . 37 cents on this smoothie today?"

Clerk: "That's right!"

Me: "Mmmmmm. Pass." This was almost as much fun as dealing with the poor little thing at Bath & Body Works earlier. She had apologized profusely for telling me that soaps were $3.50 each.

"I'm so sorry, ma'am," she had said. "They're actually four for $10."

"But that's $2.50 each," I said gently.

"I know," she said solemnly. "I had the price wrong."

"Yes, but it's even better. $2.50 is less than $3.50."

"OMG!" she squealed. "I can't wait to tell everybody."

So, yes, it had been a frustrating day mathwise at the mall and things weren't getting any better, though I did have a nice little shopping bag full of heavenly lotions and soaps that I practically stole.

The clerk seemed genuinely upset that I wasn't going to buy the rewards membership.

She turned around, disconsolate, and began to make my strawberry smoothie. I could've sworn she was crying.

She placed it beside the cash register and I reached for my wallet. At last.

Suddenly, she perked up.

"Good news!" she said after reading something on her screen. "You have been selected to receive a free trial of *Entertainment Weekly*, *Time*, or *Better Homes & Gardens* magazines. Just fill this out (another form, this time with strawberry goo on it) and your subscription will be on its way!"

Me: "No, thanks, really. Can I just get my smoothie? It's starting to sweat worse than Tim Gunn in a Kmart."

Clerk: "Of course. But first, would you like to apply for our Frequent Smoothie Card? It's not as good as the Gold Rewards, I'm afraid, but you will get one free smoothie after you pay for the first twenty-five."

"Right now, we're getting a slow start with number one," I grumbled. "OK, if it's free, sure, I'll take it."

Clerk: "And here's a scratch-off just for coming in. You

could win anywhere from five cents to $500 just by scratch-
ing off the little berry symbols. Didja win anything?"

I, to no one's real surprise, won a "Sorry! Try Again!"

"Look, I don't want to be rude but can I just get my drink?
I don't have a gold membership, I don't want to buy magazines, and now I've got all this scratch-off crud under my
fingernails."

Clerk: "You bet! That'll be $4.45. May I have your tele-
phone number starting with area code first?"

My right hand to God, this really happened.

"No."

"Ohhhh," the clerk said, smiling. "I get it. You should
know that we don't sell your personal information to anyone
if that's what you're worried about. We just want to send
you free coupons for special offers in the mail. And if you
share your e-mail address with us, you will automatically be
entered in our grand prize sweepstakes!"

"OK," I said. "You win. I have my own Web site and you
can e-mail me directly from there. It's kind of a long address. Are you ready? You might want to write this down.
It's double-u double-u double-u dot give me my mother-
humpin' smoothie before I smash your face in dot com."

She looked genuinely hurt. Go figure. I guess someone
wasn't going to have a "berry good" afternoon after all.

5

Moral Fiber Can't Help
Your Colon

The older you get, the more fiber obsessed you become. Not me, mind you, but others. If I had a dollar for every time my Aunt Verlie told me she hasn't taken a decent dump since the Carter administration, I'd be wealthy indeed. Grossed-out, but wealthy. As it stands right now, I'm just grossed out.

People of a certain age give up any pretense that it's unseemly to discuss bowel habits in polite company. And by polite company, I mean the post office, the grocery store, the bank, even church.

"Well, it says right there in the U.S. Bible that where two or more are gathered, you can talk about this stuff," says Verlie. She's gotten a little dotty lately and tends to put "U.S." in front of everything.

"I was at the U.S. Post Office," she starts and I can't resist saying, "What? Not the Mexican Post Office? You sure?"

Oh, don't judge me. Verlie would worry the shit out of a septic tank, and taking her around town on her errands because her grown son is a male-type person and therefore unable to be of any use whatsoever to an aging relative, has given me plenty of hours in the car to hear about her "piles" as she calls them. Apparently this was popular vernacular for hemorrhoids in, oh, 1817.

"It's just a U.S. nuisance is what it is," said Verlie one day after I'd picked her up from her eye doctor appointment. We were on the way to Walmart, where I knew she would demand to see the butcher and discuss which meats would be easier on her colon.

"I don't think Walmart has a butcher," I said. "It's just some guy who puts out the pretty little cellophane-wrapped packages."

"Well, he'll know what's what," she huffed. "He can recommend some U.S. meat for me."

I tell Verlie that she should be more concerned about fruits and vegetables for fiber and maybe even ease up on the meat consumption, but she just gives me a sideways look that conveys the obvious: "If you know so damn much, why does your ass hang off either side of the bucket seats in your Mustang, little missy?"

Even so.

I convinced Aunt Verlie to try a few high-fiber cereals, which did seem to help with The Problem for a while.

But all cereal is not created equal and it wasn't a surprise to me when someone blew the whistle on those wacky cereal companies whose claims were getting kinda silly, even to Verlie.

Like the "miracle tonic" salesmen who hoodooed an unsophisticated prairie public, the folks at Kellogg's even claimed that, yes, Froot Loops were good for you.

It's not even real froot! How could it possibly be good for you? And what is froot anyway?

General Mills was just as bad, practically claiming that Cheerios could cure male pattern baldness *and* give you X-ray vision.

I imagine the FDA cracked down on some of the more outlandish claims.

And, somewhere, there were real humans who were actually shocked that they got busted. I dreamed up this little conversation one day while waiting for Verlie to get her "hairs done" as she likes to say. Her son was on a cruise to St. Lucia. He's an asshole.

Kellogg's bigshot: "So you say we're not going to be allowed to claim that Frosted Mini-Wheats improve a child's attention span by 20 percent?"

Company attorney: "That's right. Because, in point of fact, that's just kind of, uh, made up."

Kellogg's BS: "I hear you. What if we say that if you eat Frosted Mini-Wheats, you will improve your IQ by twenty points? How 'bout we say that?"

Attorney: "No."

Kellogg's BS: "So I'm guessing the whole leaping tall buildings in a single bound is out, too?"

Attorney: "Rightaroonie."

Kellogg's BS: "And we really have to sign something saying that we won't make misleading claims on our cereal boxes anymore?"

Attorney: "Yes, that's the gist of it."

Kellogg's BS: "But what about the claim that Cocoa Krispies will help support your child's immune system? We can still say that, right? I mean this *is* still America the last time I looked."

Attorney: "Nope, you can't say that because it's technically not true. Eating cereals that contain up to 50 percent sugar don't keep your kid from getting colds or anything else. We just, sorta, made it up."

Kellogg's BS: "But cereal *is* good for you! It has vitamins and fiber. People love fiber! Look! I have a letter here from a woman in North Carolina . . . Verlie something . . . says that, until lately, she hasn't had a decent . . ."

Attorney: "Doesn't matter."

Kellogg's BS: "OK. But did you know that it has been clinically proven that if you eat a bowl of Frosted Flakes every day you'll never get cancer?"

Attorney: "No, it hasn't."

Kellogg's BS: "Yeah, I know."

After Verlie's hairs were done, she sank back into the front seat of my car, pushing my right thigh a bit more than necessary as she buckled up.

"Mercy!" she said. "Aren't you uncomfortable in this small car? You ought to get one of those Hummers like my Fielding drives. (But of course.) He says it's real comfortable, although I haven't ridden in it myself. Field says he doesn't want to get the floor mats dirty yet."

Suddenly, she brightened.

"Let's go to KFC," she said. "It's American, you know."

Do I ever! I once went out of my way to visit the Louisville, Kentucky, museum that honors the late Colonel Harland Sanders. There was even an animatronic likeness to gaze upon.

I asked her why she wanted to go there, because she usually complains that fried foods cause her to be "bound." Don't ask.

"The man on TV said that we should unthink KFC," Verlie said, fishing for a coupon in the bottom of her trusty Vera Bradley Hipster, perhaps the most poorly named product ever.

Verlie is very big on Vera Bradley because if there's one thing she hates worse than not crapping regularly, it's a "too-heavy pocketbook." I have heard this many hundreds of times. A heavy purse makes her cranky.

"Fielding says I shouldn't wear anything but Vera Bradley," Verlie said. "My Field says that a heavy pocketbook could cause me to lose my balance and fall down and break my hip and then where would I be?"

Probably not anywhere near Field's house, I thought. Look, I know that there are devoted, helpful sons out there who tend to their ailing, aging moms and dads but I'm not talking about those two. I'm talking about Field, who it was just like to toss out something like "Vera Bradley" when he probably just overheard it in an airport somewhere. Did I mention Field is an asshole?

But Verlie, for all her annoying quirks and uncooperative colon, deserves better, so if she needed to unthink her fast-food chicken, then I was all in.

As we scanned the new grilled menu at KFC, I couldn't help but think it was weird, like going to the International House of Pancakes and discovering that it was really just Wisconsin and a couple of Dakotas.

The name didn't even fit anymore. I could picture Colonel Sanders' animatronic statue at the museum coming alive just like Teddy Roosevelt in *Night at the Museum* (the first one, not the shitty sequel) to demand an explanation. Something along the lines of "WTF, KFC?"

Verlie said she'd buy mine, too, because one of her church circle friends had printed out some free chicken coupons from the Oprah show Web site.

That's so Oprah. Bless her heart, she honestly believes that we still care what she weighs. Oprah is crazy about the new grilled chicken at KFC. She spent a whole show pushing that chicken and put those free coupons on the "interweb" for Verlie and her friends to try.

Sadly, as I told Verlie over a Snack Pack with slaw, this led to a riot in the streets of Manhattan. When I saw investment bankers and fashion industry bigwigs slugging it out in the streets for a free wing and thigh dinner, I realized the economy really might not bounce back. Police were called, I told Verlie. Fistfights ensued. Ugly words were hollered. It was like watching an old *Springer* show without the white-trash chick with the muffin top spilling over her Gloria Vanderbilt-Dollar Tree jeans while yanking out her boyfriend's new lover's weave. Yeah. It was just like that.

Verlie was only half paying attention to me. I think she thinks I talk way too much and maybe I do.

Finally she said that we should send a thank-you note to Oprah for the free chicken, and I said I'd get right on that.

Verlie said she would've saved the coupon for Fielding but he doesn't like to eat in fast-food places because there are too many "U.S. lowlifes" hanging around.

Right. Better his cousin should take his aged mama to those sorts of places. I ordered some stress-related banana pudding and knew I'd get "the look" for having done so when we got back in the car.

"You could stand to eat a few more vegetables," Verlie said, rather pointedly I thought. "Even Michelle Obama, the

U.S. first lady, is planting a garden right there at the White House. Don't you think it's so wonderful how she's trying so hard to get all those fat little public school children in Washington to eat right?"

Well, of course I do, but, as I told Verlie, it irks me on some level when I read about Michelle Obama and Julia Roberts composting and planting gardens. Are there any other ways that brilliant, successful women can make the rest of us feel like slugs? Isn't it enough that I *buy* fresh produce, but now I gotta grow it myself? Using composting advice from a movie star?

"Oh, you're just getting yourself all worked up," said Verlie, who was working on her gums with a toothpick. "You do that all the time, you know. It's probably the menopause. When I got that, I was always running off at the mouth about every little thing."

"Watch it, Aunt Verlie!" I said. "There's a speed bump coming up and you could give yourself a lobotomy."

"My Fielding says you can get heart problems from dirty gums. A word to the wise, little missy."

"What I'm saying, Aunt Verlie, is that we women are always finding ourselves one step forward and two steps back. It's never going to be enough no matter how much we do because if the wife of the leader of the free world and the most bankable actress in Hollywood can do it, why can't we? Let me just put hoeing and weeding on the chore list this week. It just *never, ever stops being enough and I'm tired!*"

Verlie looked shocked at my outburst.

"Oh, honey, you're upset. Everybody knows those women don't actually do all that stuff themselves. Fielding says Joe Biden probably tends that garden 'cause that's all he's got the brains to do."

"Your son is a moron," I said. Uh-oh. Did I just say that out loud?

Fortunately Verlie was too distracted to hear me. I definitely didn't want to get into a political argument with Aunt Verlie, who voted for Fred Thompson in the Republican primary because he'd "won so many cases on *Law & Order.*" Plus she has a maddening habit of describing Barack Obama as "clean and articulate," as though this was somehow a surprise.

"Well, he's really a nationalized American, you know," she said, whispering the word "nationalized."

"It's a wonder he can even speak the English language as well as he does! I give him credit for that. In fact, he's a credit to his . . ."

"Stop it right there, Aunt Verlie!"

On the way home, Verlie managed to dig out yet another free-chicken-dinner coupon from the depths of her beloved Vera Bradley purse.

"Look! I found another one! Now I can take Field out, too. Maybe he'll appreciate it more than you did. You seem a little wrought up today. I'll bet you're constipated. . . ."

6

Twitter Woes: I've Got Plenty of Characters, Just No Character

A s a Southerner, one of the hardest things I've had to do lately is learn how to "tweet." Because everyone knows that Southerners lean toward being a bit long-winded, verbose, wordy, overwrought, and dense when it comes to written communication. So this means that I've had a tough time joining the Twittersphere.

How is it possible for me, *me,* to condense what I've got to say into 140 lousy characters? For the longest time, I thought it was 140 *words,* which already cramped my style plenty, but then I noticed that every time I "hauled off and tweeted" (as we say in the South), the cursor wouldn't budge beyond a couple of short sentences. Characters, it turns out, means letters. Who knew? Everybody did? Oh.

At first I just couldn't do it. We Southerners are known

for telling long, looping stories stuffed with color and pageantry and pork fat. Twitter had me communicating with friends and family in something just a little more sophisticated than a series of keyboard grunts. I felt as if everything I typed was coming out like Karl in *Sling Blade*. Mmmm-huh.

Clearly, I'd just have to adjust. After all, brevity is the soul of wit, said Shakespeare, who, methinks, would've sucked loudly at tweeting.

After the first few weeks I started getting the hang of it. It's all about self-editing. When I can convey the thought in exactly 140 characters, my day is off to a good start. Writing less seems like cheating.

I have lots of friends who tweet and most of their tweets are super boring. Some are high-minded, choosing only to tweet about things like (yawn) social justice and (bigger yawn) how precious their kids are. One friend recently posted: *Courage is being willing to walk in darkness while shining a light for others to follow.*

That's beautiful, isn't it? Compare and contrast with my tweet that day: *Just rewatched St. Elmo's Fire. Can't believe Demi Moore really thought she could kill herself by leaving the windows up on a cold night.*

My very first tweet ever was equally shallow: *A little redneck girl in line behind me at Marshall's pointed at my ass and said, "Look at the big butt, Meemaw." My life is complete.* I've learned to appreciate the way Twitter forces you to choose your words carefully. In that way, it is like haiku, the fine Japanese art of hair weaving in thirteen words, or something like that.

Another tweet informed my followers that when I die, I want my favorite words in the whole world to be inscribed on my gravestone: *Possession arrow belongs to Carolina*. I'm not kidding.

I tend to tweet about pop-culture trends and personal failings, not so much about what I just ate and similar rubbish.

As in: *Deliver me from one more headline telling me that Valerie Bertinelli lost all that weight "one day at a time."*

Lots of people give great tweet but I quickly de-follow anybody who just posts those annoying self-serving messages about whatever they're selling. That's just tacky. Unless, of course, it's me telling my followers that it's time to ante up for the new book. That's, somehow, different. That's just savvy marketing, which is strongly encouraged by my tech-savvy publisher. And by "strongly encouraged" I mean that if I don't, there have been idle threats that my next book will come out via fortune cookie.

I don't have a lot of followers but I do so love the term. I like to picture all seven hundred of mine (so far!) sitting around their computers and smart phones wearing long flowing white robes and chanting my name over and over like a calming mantra . . . Celia, Celia, Celia. . . . Isn't that what followers do?

My goal is to have as many followers (thirty thousand and

countin') as celebrity-supermodel-turned-diet-and-decorating-mogul-turned-spiritual-advisor Kathy Ireland, who, for reasons I can't imagine, was a follower of mine for a brief time. Apparently, Kathy was offended by one of my tweets, which was fine with me.

Not unlike professional loudmouth Kathy Griffin, I believe there's no such thing as bad publicity. If a big-time spokesmodel for spirituality and finer accent lighting like Kathy Ireland slams me in the Twittersphere, that is A-OK, with me. In fact, it's better than A-OK; it is awesome. This ranks right up there with the time I stayed in the room next to Cyndi Lauper at a Dallas hotel. What? I already told you about that? Well, no matter.

So Kathy got all Zen on me saying that I should lift up rather than put down or some shit like that. Oh, yeah? At least I don't make my followers drink only fermented cactus juice and take on many wives or husbands like she does. Kidding! Kathy, this is the sort of thing we in the humor biz call "hyperbole." It's not pronounced the way it looks so don't expect to go to Pottery Barn and find a set of hypercups and hypersaucers. It means exaggerating for effect.

I wish I could remember the exact tweet that hacked off the divine Ms. Ireland, who put me in my place while noting that she was just settling into her seat in first class and feeling all positive and gooey until she read something snarky that I had written.

Again, I'm way more tickled that she read it than the fact that she hated it. This woman tweets continuously, probably even while she's answering nature's call.

I'm sure Kathy Ireland is utterly delightful in a detached, obnoxiously slender kind of way but she might wanna not take everything quite so seriously. We get that she's a model *and* smart. Strangely, this doesn't surprise us as much as it seems to surprise her.

Anyway, I think I could learn a lesson from Kathy because she is just so damn chatty in her constant tweets. She's not a lazybones like me when it comes to tweeting. Seems like she must spend her entire day keeping her followers informed of every nuance of her day and, at the end of the day, she always tells her "angels" that she's going to sign off.

Goodnight, angels! she'll tweet. It's nothing short of amazing that she can take the time to do that *and* find the time to be the face in front of the designs actually created by probably hundreds of highly talented gay males.

Besides becoming more active in the Twittersphere, it has also been strongly suggested that I should increase my Internet presence by writing a daily blog.

Sigh.

Sigh again.

And once more.

What can I tell y'all? If you write all day, writing a blog just seems like one more thing to do. Must we "stream" our lives constantly? When you're constantly telling everyone exactly what you're doing (*Pot roast tonight!*) or how you're feeling (*My boss is an arrogant twit!*) it starts sounding kinda samey, right?

Because we are all so conscious of blabbing our every thought these days, it's no wonder some of us are saying a little too much.

Consider Twitter-savvy Senator Chuck Grassley of Iowa's suggestion that AIG executives should either resign or take a deep bow and *follow the Japanese example of killing themselves*. Grassley did this as easily and lightly as if he had suggested that he'd be happy to bring the lime Jell-O mold to the Senate picnic.

In a separate but related story, Judge Judy said recently that she was surprised that the loathsome Bernie Madoff didn't kill himself rather than go to prison. I ask you: Is that any way for an officer of the make-believe television court to talk?

My point is that we might need to be more circumspect in the face of all this chattiness.

As one who receives quarterly "benefits" statements from AIG (which stands for "all I got" in my case), I should be as angry as anybody about dozens of soulless suits receiving millions of dollars in bonuses for doing The Worst Job in the History of the Working World, but I believe that the rules of polite society dictate that we should never, ever invite anyone to off himself, even in jest.

No, no. It would be far more gratifying to see a few AIG

bigwigs dropped off in *Deliverance*land dressed only in silver lame 'chaps and I (HEART) GUN CONTROL LAWS T-shirts.

I know—goosebumps, right?

Lately, in my real, not cyber, life, I've had an unusually hard time holding my tongue, and I believe it's because I'm so used to cyber-sharing too much that I've forgotten how to turn it off.

And while I haven't invited the lunkhead who double billed me for a repair and refused to refund the money to do the honorable thing and plunge a samurai sword through his chest, I did toy with the notion.

As a Southerner, this conduct is simply unbecoming. We are famous for avoiding telling people they have displeased us in any way and will go to outlandish lengths to dance around unpleasant scenes. Except we don't anymore. And I'm a little freaked out about that.

So, yes, I will try to be more positive, just like Kathy Ireland said I should be. I don't want to be the kind of person who only tells the clerk at the DMV that I'm an organ donor because everybody else is doing it. (Well, everybody else was saying "Yes!" with so much enthusiasm, I was afraid they were going to whip out their livers and lay 'em on the desk right then and there. I just said "Yes" so everybody else in line wouldn't mutter "Selfish porkface. Can you believe she's keeping her organs? Like they're so freakin' special. . . . Ooooh, like she thinks her spleen is all that.")

I want to be a better person like probable-organ-donor

Miss Kathy Ireland! Perhaps this will lead to greater success; it certainly seems to have worked for her. I still fly coach, after all.

But, really, how does one define success?

I'll tell you how I don't define it.

I don't define success by how much money someone makes. I don't define success by how many trophies or plaques or awards someone has.

I don't define it by membership in exclusive clubs or the ability to name-drop about someone's famous friends.

I don't define it by how many luxury cars or opulent homes someone might own or how many sumptuous vacations they might take in exotic locales all over the globe.

I don't define success . . . oh, hell, I'm just kidding. Actually, all that stuff is *fantastic!*

But enough of all that chatter. It's time to say "Nighty night" to all of my angels.

Yeah, that felt weird.

7

Bitter! Party of Me

Now that Oprah Winfrey has announced the end of her long-running talk show, who, pray tell, is going to scream the names of celebrities in that annoying fashion? You know what I'm talking about: "Ladies and gentlemen . . . JOHN TRAVOOOOOLLLLLTTTTAAAA!"

And who is going to give hour-long shout-outs to thick, thoughty novels that make my head hurt when I read them?

No one? Oh, OK.

As loyal readers know, I have sent my books to "Noprah" for many years now. Frankly, as native Southerners who share having grown up in towns so small they could best be described as "two stores, two whores, and a cotton gin," Oprah and I should have a lot in common. I was expecting that at least she'd send me an autographed picture or something.

("To Celia, from OOOOOPPPPPRRRRRAAAAAHH-HHH!") But nada, bupkiss, zilch. So to Oprah, let me just say thanks for, uh, nothing.

O has clearly forgotten that Southerners always send thank-you notes. There's more than a grain of truth to the old joke that the only reason Southern Junior Leaguers don't participate in orgies is that there would be too many thank-you notes to write.

Oprah received a gift from me—several, actually—over the years and still no note. To put it in terms she can understand, there are "NOOOO EXCUUUUUUSES!" and that includes (but is not limited to) such afflictions as "Thoughtless Billionaire Syndrome," "Yes I'm All That-osis," or even "My Vah-jay-jay's on the Fritz and I Can't Be Bothered-itis."

Oh, I just hate sounding so bitter. But *ten* years of mailing books to my Southern sister has taken its psychic toll. How I dreamed of sitting across from O on one of those big, puffy yellow chairs she uses for the cry-interviews.

How I'd envisioned in my fevered dreams of nonfiction stardom how our conversation would go:

O: "So tell us about your books, Celia."

Me: "Well, I . . ."

O: "But first, did you know that your daughter has the same name as my beloved late dog, Sophie? Did you name your daughter after my dog? Did you? I bet you did! (*turning toward audience*) "YOU get a dog and YOU get a dog and YOU get a dog!"

Me: "Actually, Oprah, I'm more of a cat person."

O: "Ladies and gentlemen, MAYA ANGELOOO-OUUUU!"

Me: "What?!?"

O: "She's going to be our guest tomorrow. I'm just warming up."

Me: "Yes, well, you see I write humor, some of it is pop-culture based but always with a Southern subtext and . . ."

O: "OK, here's the part of the interview where I just start randomly interrupting you so we can talk about me some more. Hey! What does your poo look like? Dr, Oz says mine is perfect!"

Me: "Yes, I saw that show. You truly have no secrets."

O: "Oh, but I do! I have *the* Secret! You just think your way to success by putting all the good thoughts out there into the universe."

Me: "You know that's a bunch of crap, right?"

O: (*sighing*) "Yeah, but people eat it up like pie on Sunday."

Me: (*distracted*) "Mmmmm, pie . . ."

O: "Join us tomorrow when Maya Angelou and I will discuss the politics of being happy and dogs and Skype and child-molesting and holiday decorations for less. . . ."

I realize how petty it must sound to constantly complain that O hasn't done me a solid.

But I've been in this writing business for a while. I've paid my dues and I've been a mentor for dozens of aspiring writers. And by mentor I mean, I've told them not to be jerks and quit their day jobs.

The truth is that you don't go into this business for the money. You go into writing because you can't imagine doing anything else, because the words wake you up at night and, most important of all, because it's probably the only job in the whole world you could do while seated on the toilet.

People often ask me, "How come you don't sweat much for a fat girl?" No, no, that's not what I meant to say. Although it is so totally true and, in fact, it is what I am most proud of in this life. I mean raising a child to be a kind, caring, and productive member of society is fine, but this low-sweat thing is a Really Big Deal, just saying.

No, what I meant to say is that they ask me how I stay so disciplined. Writing can be such a solitary business that it's not for everyone. And you have to be prepared to steel yourself against all the inevitable distractions when you work at home.

For instance, just this morning, I have become preoccupied with trying not to take it as a bad omen that, for the past three hours, there has been a white, adult-sized casket sitting on the back of a flatbed truck parked right in front of my house.

It's just sitting there. No driver, no sign of life, *ha-ha*, just sitting out there in front of my house, gleaming in the sunshine with its little carved white rosettes on the sides.

OK, I believe you can see how easy it is to get off-task unless you use a few tricks to stay focused on your writing. But *you* try to concentrate with a casket staring at you all morning.

Oh, hell, here comes the garbage truck. If whoever belongs with that white casket messes up my once-a-week pickup and I have to smell these shrimp shells for another second, I'll personally dig her up and kill her all over again.

Then again, it could be that one of my neighbors just bought a casket "for later." You can get them at Costco and Sam's Club you know. Right there beside the hundred-count packages of Pork-On-A-Stick.

Oh my God, where was I?

Yes, yes, disciplined writing. I think it's a good idea to write at least ten pages a day. I mean, I've never done that but it sounds like a really good place to start, doesn't it?

Once you've gotten published, it's important not to let it go to your head. Don't do dumb stuff like, if somebody calls you by your first name, say: "That's *mister* Asshole to you," or whatever. People hate that.

It's very important, karma-wise, to always be willing to give a hand up to another writer whenever, however, you can. Naturally, this doesn't apply if the writer is better than you. I mean, that's food off your table, you feel me?

The truth? I've always wanted to be one of those classy writers that heaps genuine praise on all my published friends. I want to gush and ooze heartfelt wishes that their Amazon ranking never rises above a thousand. I want to be that person, but it's hard. The truth is that I am always a bit jealous when a writer friend's book does better than mine. Which happens a lot, since you ask.

Sometimes, though, I try to do the right thing. I'll give you an example: A couple of years ago, I was attending the Southern Independent Booksellers Alliance convention in Orlando. About fifteen of us author-types were doing what amounted to speed dating. We'd already speed eaten a couple of tiny ham and cheese on yeast roll thingies before being told to work the crowd, spending exactly ten minutes at each table, charming and chatting up bookstore owners from across the Southeast.

All the other authors were familiar to me. We'd traveled in the same circles more than once. It wasn't, as they say, my first trip to the rodeo.

But there was a shy, quiet fellow at our authors' table. As we wolfed our minisubs and got ready to rumble, I decided it was my Christian duty to make this man feel welcome. I dragged him into the table conversation but he barely made eye contact. Poor lil fella, I thought. He's so overwhelmed by all of us big shots. Clearly, he was a book-convention virgin.

Is it enough to say that I talked the poor man's ears off, sharing my sorta-vast knowledge of all things regional book tour? Is it enough to say that he listened quietly and politely even, at one point smiling a tiny bit?

Is it enough to say that all of a sudden, the chairman of the convention walked up and began to talk to the poor soul, earnestly complimenting him on his Pulitzer *and* his National Book Award?

Oh, I thought, now realizing that on top of everything else, I'd been talking to him with a big mustardy bread crumb affixed to my bottom lip. Just let me take my impossibly dumb ass and lumber across the room to charm the book buyers, who by now were all atwitter about having such a distinguished guest in their midst. Him, not me; pay attention.

I'm not being small when I say I can't recall the man's name. They say the mind forgets truly intense pain.

Since that awful day, I've chatted up a few famous author-types including David Sedaris and the late John Updike. And, no, I didn't ask Updike to detail my car or mistake Sedaris for a hungry drifter and offer to buy him a Hardee's Thickburger, which, let's be honest, he really looks like he could use, bless his precious nicotine-ravaged heart.

I did give Sedaris an advance copy of my book and asked him if he would consider, pretty please, writing a tiny blurb. It would mean so much, I stammered. And by so much, I was already thinking ahead to how, if I sold enough books, we might finally be able to afford to close in a porch off our bedroom and make it into a huge walk-in closet because, as I told "Dave," we have virtually no closet space in our ninety-year-old fixer-upper and I know how gay men can sympathize with something as heart wrenching as an abysmal lack of sufficient closet space.

He listened to this with an air of amused detachment, as though, in his mind, he was already back at his French villa with his lovah, Hugh, sipping Turkish coffee and pondering his next seven-figure advance.

Yes, just a couple of words from Sedaris and my life could change forever.

When I finally shut up, he, as nicely as any human could ever do it, looked me in the eye and said "No." David Sedaris explained that, basically, he got requests like mine all the time and he only writes blurbs for two authors a year, and then only for people he knows personally.

"But I'm in your genre! You might even like it! *I will pay you whatever you want.* Do you want the shiny hairs?!" It was humbling to realize that, food chain-wise, it was my turn to be the woman with the listing Bumpit and the man with the shiny black pants.

And then, just as quickly as he'd appeared, David Sedaris was ushered away to his next book-tour stop and I stood alone in the lecture hall at the local college, feeling very small and insignificant. Rather like I imagine his wingwang to be.

Three years ago, my book made it to the final five in a national humor-writing contest. Sedaris won. Did he remember the nervous but curiously nonsweating woman from his very own North Carolina who had tried to press that book into his bony little hand-claws just one short year ago?

Oh, I'm sure not.

Ditto another book a couple of years later. Oh? What's

this? You really think Jon Stewart and his gazillion-member staff is more deserving? Well, go on with your bad self.

This past summer, my most recent book made it to the top three in the category of Best Nonfiction Book of the Year in the South.

But what's this? Another Pulitzer winner beat the snot out of me to take that one? And, yes, I hate him just a little bit. Kidding! I'm sure he's a delightful fellow and there is absolutely no truth to the rumor that, below the neck, he is covered entirely in scales.

Oh, high road, you're just so very overrated.

8

Road Trip to Nuh-what-kah
Rouses Suspicions

Nebraska—that's one of the rectangular states out west known for corn and, well, corn—has been in the news lately because its "safe haven" law, as written, allows people to drop off not just unwanted newborns, but even surly teenagers for someone else to take care of.

All together now: "Suh-weet!"

Things got so bad that Nebraska governor Dave ("Hiney man") Heineman was forced to call a news conference in which he actually pleaded, "Please don't bring your teenager to Nebraska."

One state is simply not equipped to handle that much sass, I guess. There is, after all, no Undersecretary of Attitude, or Department of Demanding Money While At the Same Time Screaming At You to Get Out of My Life.

Who knew?

Turns out that once the word leaked that the Nebraska safe haven law has a loophole the size of, well, Nebraska, parents from across the country tossed their unruly teens into the car, and took them for a long ride in the country, so to speak.

While the governor and others have said they'd just love to take care of every one of the little cherubs, they, uh, have to wash their hair that night or something and have decided to change the law.

But not in time to prevent parents from as far away as Florida and Georgia from dumping their teens at Nebraska's finer hospital.

I'm guessing those were some pretty tense road trips.

Surly Teen (waking and stretching and removing iPod ear buds for the first time since approximately 2004): "So where did you say we were going?"

Frazzled Parent: "Hmmmm? Oh, just for a nice long ride in the country. Where there is a huge meadow with a big barn and you can catch all the mice you need."

ST: "Whaaaa?"

FP: "Oh, sorry, I was distracted. That's what we did with the cat, but this is going to be much better than that. You're going to live in *Nebraska*! Isn't that wonderful?"

ST: "Nuh-what-kah?"

FP (*nervously*): "You love corn, right?"

Of course, these parents didn't get to this point over-night. As the mama of a middle schooler, I can tell you it's scary out there. The Princess is in seventh grade, you re-member. The other day she was telling me about a fight on the playground between two eighth-grade boys.

"Who are they?" I asked, looking around the school yard.

"I don't know 'em personally," she said. "But I do know one of them has a beard. And a son."

Holy crap!

Hard to believe that it wasn't all that long ago that the biggest worry shared by teachers, parents, and students was whether or not the eggs warming under the light bulb in the kindergarten room's incubator were going to hatch into fluffy yellow chicks before the kids left for spring break.

A beard. And a son.

This was right after a conversation with a friend whose kid goes to a middle school across town.

It seems the dad was volunteering to help with bus duty when he gently asked a petite sixth-grade girl to wait for traffic to clear before she darted across the street to join her friends.

"Shut up, dickhead," she said, staring him down. "You're not the boss of me!"

Whoa. You eat Happy Meals with that mouth?

Yoo hoo! Nebraska! Table for one, please.

But that's not all! Leaving a school concert one night, I

was shocked to hear one of the seventh graders yelling into her cell phone, "If you can't pick me up, then stay your ass home, Grandma."

When a student shoved me aside to buy tickets at a football game at Sophie's school one afternoon, I started to demand an apology.

"Mama, don't mess with her," said the Princess, putting her hand on my arm protectively.

"Why? She just broke in line! No cuts!"

"She once shot a man in Reno just to watch him die."

"Oh, for God's sake, honey, that's a Johnny Cash song."

"I know," she hissed. "I had to put it in terms that even you would understand. She's been to juvie!"

This was nuts. Did she really think I was going to be afraid of some seventh-grade girl?

"So what?" I told the Princess as we edged closer to the ticket booth. "I've watched every season of *Oz*. She can't scare me. Watch and learn."

OK, so the girl turned around right about then and gave me a look that made me nearly, well, I believe the technical term for it is pee myself.

One of the most important life lessons any parent can impart is the importance of choosing one's battles, as I later explained to an overly smug Princess.

"Where's all your big talk now?" she teased.

"Darling, it's quite obvious to me that my shoulder was in that nice girl's way. Bad shoulder!"

Nebraska is big, but is it big enough to contain the two teenage girls I saw pulling out each other's hair during a cat-fight over a boy?

I mean, the only pair of size eight Marc Jacobs orange leather platform sandals at DSW, that's one thing, but a *boy*? Puleez. The world is so full of those.

Frankly, I think the world would be better if every parent treated their kid the way Betty Draper does on *Mad Men*.

At her terse command to "Go upstairs," Betty's children wordlessly untangle their legs, stand up, turn off the TV and go upstairs.

Not even so much as a "Just two more hours of Mario Kart, puleeeez." (Although, to be fair, the show is set in 1963 so it's not like the kids are being asked to give up that much.)

Betty Draper talks to her kids like that all the time, even if the table is set for dinner and you know the kids will have to amuse themselves for hours while she swirls a drink at the kitchen table with moody husband Don, and smokes a ciga-rette or twelve.

And there's more from the Betty Draper School of Par-enting.

When the kids are outside playing and it's time to get cleaned up, Betty steps onto the front porch, puts her hands on her hips and says, "Go inside." *And they do!* No back talk. No eye rolls. No negotiations.

Sure, Betty "Drano" is harsh and even a little toxic to her

kids by today's standards but I'm pretty sure her son would never be a baby-daddy in eighth grade.

She often looks at her children with utter curiosity, as if she can't quite figure out how these short people came to live in her house. But then I have to realize that things were different then. Parents said what they wanted; children, mostly, complied—an unthinkable notion in this kid-centric age.

Betty Draper would never tolerate a boy named Artemis Battlestar or some such with tangled shoulder-length curls and a stained favorite T-shirt pledging allegiance to a greener planet.

She'd merely level her imperious gaze at him and say, "Change your clothes."

And following that, "Tell your father to take you to the barber. You look like a very unattractive girl."

Although I could never be as flat-out mean as Betty Draper, it would be fab to just one time have my will be done. I tried to channel Betty the other day.

Standing at the Princess' bedside, I smoothed my vintage apron, folded my arms across my chest, and tapped my high-heel-clad foot before flicking a wayward shred of imaginary tobacco from my front tooth.

"Get up," I said, trying to emulate that soft-but-scary way Betty talks to her kids.

Nothing. Not even a slight rustle of the covers, despite the fact that the alarm clock had gone off ten minutes earlier.

"Get up!"

A gentle stirring, then a muffled, "I don't wanna go to school."

WWBD?

"I'm going to get your father."

Too late. She was already asleep again. Betty Draper makes it look so damn easy through her Miltown-induced cold-calm parenting.

"GET UP!!!!!!"

I look up, helplessly, at Adam Lambert's grinning face above the bed. On the opposite wall was Vampire heartthrob Taylor Lautner, looking equally amused at my plight.

After a minute or so, I sighed deeply and walked out, defeated.

"Jiminy, what a pussy," I could hear Betty Draper hiss.

Betty would've loved to drop her kids in Nebraska, but really, why should parents have all the fun?

Why not drop off every asshole who's tried to ruin your life over the years? I'm talking deadbeat dads, shiftless spouses, no-account boyfriends, cheatin' girlfriends, the cast of *Jersey Shore*, even that jerk of a boss of yours—all under the guise of going to see the World's Largest Ball of Stamps.

Pesky magazine salesman at your door?

Grab your keys and ask, "Hey! Would you like to see the motel room that was trashed by Michael Landon in 1962? It's in fabulous Neligh, Nebraska!"

Auto mechanic rip you off? It's time to visit Carhenge, an amazing Stonehenge replica made entirely from junked cars and located in picturesque Alliance, Nebraska.

There's so much more to lure the baggage in your life away to Nebraska. Do I really need to say more than "Expertly taxidermied hundred-year-old two-headed calf?" I thought not.

Personally, I'm trying not to be suspicious that duh-hubby recently suggested *completely out of the blue* that we take a cross-country trip to Nebraska.

"That's great!" I said. "I know Sophie would love to see the Shoe Fence. I've read that it goes on for miles and it's covered with all kinds of shoes and boots."

But Duh held his hand up to stop me in mid quirky-shoe-display swoon.

He said Soph wouldn't be going, which was a little suspicious since she's the one who has always dreamed of seeing a fence covered with old athletic shoes. OK, maybe that was me.

Also, the time of year made his choice suspicious.

"But isn't Nebraska really cold at this time of year?" I asked. "I mean, it's January. I don't even think the Kool-Aid man exhibit is open this month. I don't want to go if it's so cold I can't enjoy standing in the giant footsteps of Kool-Aid man, like the guidebook says."

"Nonsense," said Duh, but then he seemed to soften a bit. "Well, I suppose it can get a bit crisp out there. Hmmmm.

Maybe you should pack a *lot* of clothes. That way, you can always layer things if it gets too chilly. Say some summer shirts under a few coats and sweaters. Oh, and don't forget to pack your medications."

Yeah, I'm worried.

9

Breakfast with Fabolous

When you're on the road plugging a book, you never know who you'll meet on those morning TV shows like *Wake Up, Watauga!* or *The Breakfast Club with Biff & Susie.*

I've done a lot of these shows over the years even though I truly detest that o-dark-thirty time frame. I've learned that you want to arrive early so you can spend plenty of time luxuriating in the stale coffee smell of the green room, which is almost never green. You pass the time nervously chatting with another guest, usually a local chef who's going to cook something that nobody should have to smell at six in the morning but is probably great later in the day.

One time, my only friend in the green room was an orangutan and its keeper. While you might be thinking *Oh, how cute!*, you should know that I spent the whole time being irrationally pissed that the monkey's hair was totally better looking than mine. "Pantene" had tons of silken hair and I coveted it. The orangutan took such a liking to me that during my interview segment, he sprang from his owner's arms and jumped into my lap, coyly looking up at me while I tried to ignore him.

Here's a tip: You can't ignore an orangutan. It's damn near impossible. At one point, he became fascinated with my earring and tried to eat it. They should tell you stuff like "Don't wear shiny jewelry in case a monkey wants to eat you" when you sign up for these shows.

So while the host and I tried valiantly to talk about my book and pretend there wasn't a monkey gnawing on my earlobe, it wasn't what you'd call easy. At one point I wanted to say, "Look, I don't want to overstate the obvious here, but there is a *monkey eating my head and you don't seem to care.*"

But I'm no diva, so if my biggest fan in the world turns out to be a thirty-five-pound monkey with great hair but a bald ass, well, so be it.

Truthfully, I usually love the green room. You never know what to expect. Even a dinky TV station can have a terrific green room: a full complement of coffee and tea offerings, lighted make-up mirrors, sanitized little brushes and combs to use (mercifully the orangutan brought his own) and, in rare cases, an actual makeup person who is there to make sure you don't wash out under the lights.

Although I've been doing this a few years, I've never run

into anybody famous in the green room. That is, until I was in Atlanta to tape a morning show not long ago.

When I arrived, it was hard to miss the fleet of Escalades sitting in the parking lot, all backed in as though a quick getaway might be required.

Since my morning green room company is usually at more of a Ford Focus station wagon level of fame, I could tell something was up.

But what?

I went straight to the green room to scope things out. And by things, I mean really excellent crullers that would keep my stomach from growling during the interview. I dived in.

There was a makeup woman waiting for me and, more important, whoever belonged to all those Escalades.

Makeup lady seemed a little anxious every time the door opened.

I dusted the cruller crumbs off my skirt and sat in her chair while she distractedly applied some blush.

And then, a side door I hadn't noticed earlier cracked open a little, then swung wide. Very wide, to accommodate not one, not two, three or four but *five* very large men wearing sunglasses and Diesel jeans.

They immediately sat down in a protective circle of chairs to surround a rather slight young man wearing sunglasses and a hat pulled down low. He slumped in his chair and it was clear he didn't want to talk.

It was also clear that he was The Talent.

The bodyguards for rapper Fabolous had him safe as in his mama's womb. Good thing; he's been shot before, you know.

And then, this surreal sight: One by one, the big men pulled out white bags stacked high with Styrofoam platters of McDonald's pancakes and sausage. Watching their enormous ham hands try to open those dainty little syrup containers was priceless. Balancing the breakfast on their knees, and using lilliputian plastic knives and forks, they seemed more intent on eating than protecting their charge.

Fabolous. Right here. In front of me. And no doubt he would've been shocked silly to learn that the middle-aged white lady across from him, and wearing the hell out of a Talbot's suit, knew who he was—let alone that at that moment I was furiously texting my tween that I was "having breakfast with Fabolous, so in . . . your . . . face!"

Of course, a conversation was going to be impossible. "Fab," as I like to call him, was curled up in true fetal position and seemed a little bothered by the smell of all that syrup and imitation butter surrounding him. I had the sense that he hadn't slept in a very long time.

The makeup woman fussed with her brushes and combs, probably wondering if Fab would ever get up and let her work on him but smart enough not to ask him.

In person, Fabolous looks much younger than he is. What can I tell you? I have a quirky fascination with rappers, especially the ones who've been shot.

Fab has all that, plus a pesky rumor that he had something to do with stealing a Lamborghini (it wasn't in the parking lot; I looked) and, juiciest of all, that they had recently confiscated five hundred *pounds* of marijuana from his tour bus.

Who does that? Who rides around in America with five hundred pounds of weed in their car? I mean besides Paula Deen. Fab said he didn't have anything to do with all that. Wasn't even in the tour bus, which was, no surprise here, coming back from the NBA All-Star Game. He's a good boy. OK, not really.

I mean you don't get shot up outside a nice Manhattan restaurant unless something's up. You can only play that wrong place/wrong time card so many times.

Looking at Fab sleeping so peacefully, he looked like a child, not a bad-boy East Coast gangsta rapper who uses exceedingly naughty words on occasion. For effect, of course. See, when people like me and Fab cuss, it's art. Are we clear on that now?

I was wondering how to ask the now dead-asleep Fab for his autograph or perhaps if he would pose for a cell phone picture with me, but I knew better. Even though they were completely distracted with making perfect swirlies of butter and syrup on top of their pancakes, Fab's bodyguards were big agile guys who would happily snap my arm like a Frito if I put a camera in his face. No doubt.

As I was ruminating on all this, a production assistant stuck her head in the green room and told me it was time for my segment. Which, since you ask, went a lot better than the orangutan one. The host was perky, smart, and had actually read my book, which almost never happens. Meanwhile, I was hoping that Fab and Co. were watching on the monitor in the green room and thinking that I might not be a complete loser. As the interview was winding down, I started to ask the host if I could "give a shout-out to my homeboy Fabolous waiting in the green room," but thought that might be a bit much.

I tried to hang around for a while afterward, but my driver was antsy to get to the next stop. And although I was being driven in a pretty sweet Lexus SUV, it just wasn't the same as having a bad-boy entourage of forward-facing Escalades.

"I want bodyguards and an entourage like Fabolous!" I pouted to the driver that morning.

"Who?" he asked. Oh, gawd. Could he *be* any more white and middle-aged male?

"Duhhhhh. The guy with all the cars back there. And the entourage. I mean, no offense, but all I got is you."

"So what's so bad about me?"

"Nothing, really," I said, sounding churlish even to my own ears. "But let's just say that I don't think Fabolous ever has to ride around with a hundred pounds of dog food in the back seat."

From the studio, we headed to a breakfast place, since the cruller was long gone, having been sweated away with the excitement of seeing a celebrity.

I picked at my Greek omelet and home fries and felt a little better thinking about how Fab's entourage wasn't eating anything nearly as nice as I was, so maybe things weren't so dreary after all.

So, in honor of Fabolous, who has no idea I am even alive, much less in awe of sorta meeting him, I have written a rap song.

ODE TO FABOLOUS . . .
I saw U in the A.M.
It was sorta surreal
Hangin' with your homeboys
Damn! They love a fast-food meal

CHORUS
You say your pops was lousy
The dude walked out on you
If I could bust him in the jaw
I'd do it, yeah, it's true

Yeah, I rock the Talbotwear
Boucle jacket look so hot
Judge not this book from cover, though
You don't know me from squat

I'm old enough to be your moms
But that don't mean I'm dead

Cuz cool is ageless, word it is
And smarts is in your head

CHORUS
You say your pops was lousy
The dude walked out on you
If I could bust him in the jaw
That's just what I'd do.

Copyright 2010 Talbot's Petite Gun Party Records.

10

Loonies Litter Landscape of (*snicker*) The Learning Channel

Octomom's all over the TV again, and y'all have no idea how hard I've tried to avoid screaming, "You crazy bitch!" out loud every single time I see her give an interview.

The pups are a year old as I write this, bless their tiny, still-developing hearts. I wish them lives of sunshine and rainbows and unlimited really good-quality ice cream, not the gummy cheap stuff, because, let's face it, that nutty broodmare of a mama they got is likely to try again.

I know, I know. It's none of our business if she wants to keep that clown car of a uterus of hers on go. Right you are. So why does she make me crazy?

Hmmmmm. OK, I got it! It's because she's still yakking about becoming a counselor.

OK, she's got fourteen kids, no job, and no husband, but

she's going to counsel others? This is like getting relationship advice from Chris Brown; in other words, a colossally bad idea.

Could it only have been a year ago that we were introduced to Miz Thang and her sad family? Remember how her daddy crowed that a job had just opened up for him in Iraq so he wouldn't be around to help out?

I feel ya, dude. You have to be pretty desperate to flee sunny California for Iraq *voluntarily*. But I'm guessing he'd eat sand-and-mustard sandwiches for months rather than hang out in that loony bin.

And poor Octomom's mother is probably not far behind her husband. She's probably browsing the help-wanted ads in the *Kabul Penny Saver* right about now.

Remember, she said she was "upset" when she learned that there were eight buns in the oven and they'd all be living with her in a three-bedroom house.

Upset?

No. Upset is when you do that thing where you're brushing your teeth and all of a sudden the brush goes up your nostril for no good reason. This is, well, bigger than upset.

Truth is, I struggle with this whole subject a little because it's tacky to poke fun at people who are, and I will use the clinical psychiatric term here, crazier'n a sprayed roach. It's the same way I feel guilty looking at those "People of Walmart" photos that you see on the Internet. It's not cool to make fun of pitiful people. You really think anyone who wasn't batshit crazy would walk out of the house in a camouflage mankini and a Confederate flag ball cap to go buy some new furnace filters? No, he's cray-cray.

The only joy I got out of Octomom's weird saga was how much it probably pissed off Kate Gosselin. Don't you know she was freaking out about the possibility that Octoloon was going to inherit her show?

("At least Jon and I were married. I mean, excuse my language, but criminy!")

TLC loves freaky-big families. Low TV moment of the TLC week: When Jim Bob Duggar, daddy of nineteen and counting, advised his young bridegroom son that "sex is a lot like Legos." I was hoping his bride-to-be would get wind of that and run like her clothes were on fire but, no. Like Legos? What does that even mean?

So while I'm uncomfortable snickering at people photographed while looking tacky at Walmart, I'm fine with berating those who set themselves up for publicity.

Which brings me to *The Real Housewives of New Jersey.* Y'all I had to start watching that show every week because, well, my IQ was just too high. I mean seriously up there. What can I tell you? After watching every episode, I am now officially as dumb as that brown, particle-like stuff you find outside and don't want to track inside the house. Rhymes with "wirt," I think.

The housewives are completely diverse personalities— that is, if your idea of diversity is every woman is loud, catty, big-haired or big-"bubbied" (their favorite word for breasts, don'tchaknow) and they make Fran Drescher's nasal Nanny sound like James Earl Jones.

Let me give you the skinny, in case you decide to tune in for the next season.

First, there's Caroline, the matriarch type who is kind of a low talker compared to the others. I can never quite make out what she's saying but it sounds a lot like, "If that whore lays her hands on my precious son, Albie, I'm gonna dump her bony body in the Pine Barrens, I'm just saying, yada-yada, fughedaboutit, cannoli."

To which her sister-in-law and the designated peacemaker of the bunch, Jersey wife Jacqueline, will just say, "Anyways, who wants a mani-pedi and I really want to have a third baby despite the fact that I appear to binge-drink champagne in the middle of a Wednesday afternoon. Anyways, don't judge me!"

Dina has a bored-by-it-all tone and frequently kvetches that she doesn't "have time for all the drama." Which makes me want to point out that most folks who don't have time for drama don't say that in front of a roomful of TV lights and cameras. It's possible that big-sister Caroline low-talk threatened her into doing the show. Dina is more of a faux housewife because we rarely see Mr. Dina. He's more of an idea than an actual person, I think.

Formerly flat-chested Teresa spent the first four episodes talking about how her simpleton husband, Joe, liked her the way she was and that was good enough for her. But that doesn't make for interesting TV so fast-forward a few episodes and there's Joe telling Teresa's plastic surgeon that he'd like to see her with some "full Cs." Teresa giggles and agrees to all this and now no longer weeps while trying on bikinis with the girls in Atlantic City. Oy vey.

And finally there's faux wife Danielle, whom the others hate because they think she's too skanky to hang out with women as classy as they are. There's much sniping behind backs, tearful reconciliations, and then worse sniping than ever. It's middle school all over again only with way too much leopard furniture. So, yes, I are dumber now than when I started watching those *Real Housewives*. Mission accomplice, I always say.

And just when I thought the bar couldn't get any lower (assuming Octomom doesn't get the show she dreams of), I discovered the show, *My Monkey Baby*. Not since the debut of *I Didn't Know I Was Pregnant!* have I been this excited.

This should answer, once and for all, those satellite TV ingrates who love to whine about how they have 856 channels and nothing to watch. I repeat: monkey babies.

Who could resist following the daily hijinks of Jessica Marie, a girl monkey with her own pink bedroom, designer clothes, toys, games, and makeup?

TLC, which used to stand for The Learning Channel but now stands for Titillating Losers for Cash, follows quasi-redneck couple Lori and Jim Johnson as they, seriously, examine the questions "How strong is the parent/monkey bond?"

and, my personal favorite, "Can a monkey really be a child substitute?"

TLC, sounding downright journalistic, promises that *My Monkey Baby* explores "the real lives of people parenting monkeys in America." Thank the sweet Lord above that Walter Cronkite isn't alive to see this.

Standing in the canned ravioli aisle at a Tarzana Safeway wearing ratty bedroom scuffs, the Octomom is probably slapping her forehead.

"Monkey babies! Why didn't I think of that?"

Monkey mama Lori has two grown, human daughters of her own, but apparently they were much harder to hold down and administer blush and lipstick to.

"She loves it!" coos Lori, while Jessica Marie gazes stupidly at a tube of something that was probably tested on her long-lost cousin.

I'm sorry I said "stupidly." Wouldn't want to set Jim off. He gets a might riled if you call Jessica Marie a monkey.

"Don't call her that! She's my daughter one hundred percent!"

Given his propensity to wax philosophic over a cold 'un while a cigarette bounces up and down on his lip, who am I to argue? Maybe he has the DNA test to prove it.

I smell ratings bonanza here. No, sorry. That was just Jessica Marie flinging something. But I seriously believe that TLC could craft a TV special here that melds all of its best efforts from the TLC/Discovery family.

Those wacky Duggars (see "Legosex," above) should add a few monkey babies to the mix. The only problem would be convincing the monkeys to give up their computer skills in favor of wearing gingham aprons and writing on a slate.

Or Jessica Marie, who wears pink sparkly tutus, I kid you not, could compete in the gruesomely watchable *Toddlers & Tiaras*, a show in which fathers of little-girl beauty pageant contestants dare to teach dance routines while claiming not to be gay at all.

If Jim, Jessica Marie's possible bio-dad, lurched around the corner in his wife beater at just the wrong time, those feisty *Police Women of Broward County* could wrassle him to the ground and Tase him just like they do in every show. Carmindy, the comely makeup artist from *What Not to Wear* could then wax, well, everything.

Meanwhile, with Jon and Kate's little family off the air thanks to Jon's unfortunate penchant for cheatin', the good news is that Octomom might finally get her shot.

I imaging she's licking those inflated lips of hers over the prospect.

"Did someone call for a mother of multiples who has sleek Angelina Jolie-like hair? Because I had my eight all at one time, not just six like Kate Gosselin. I mean anyone could have *six* babies at one time. Please. I could do that while I'm checking out at Costco."

So Octonut may, at last, get her close-up. Like they always

say, when one door closes, another eight or so open in the oversized custom maxi van provided by sponsors.

I'm sure the folks at TLC are only slightly jittery about replacing the Gosselins with a woman who thinks that Brad Pitt actually belongs to *her,* and I don't mean Ann Curry, bless her heart. (Note to NBC: Give Ann Curry a vacation. She touched Brad's *face* during an interview! The only people allowed to do that are Angelina and maybe George Clooney.)

Meanwhile, sad Kate Gosselin hopes to rise like a publicity-crazed phoenix from the ashes of Jon's burned and slashed Ed Hardy T-shirts (could he possibly look like more of a doofus?). She's entertaining the notion of hosting a TV talk show, which would be perfect for viewers who find Tyra too intellectually challenging.

No offense, but really, what does Kate bring to the talk-show table? I'm picturing the first week of shows based on Kate's ideas. . . .

Monday: Why Jon Cheated on Me With That Skank

Tuesday: Jon's Hairplugs Look Stupid, Don't They?

Wednesday: Jon Gosselin's a bed wetter (and other fun facts)

Thursday: All Eight Kids Tell Why They Hate Jon and Why They Think Our Bodyguard Is Way More Buff and Looks a Little Like Mark Harmon, Am I Right?"

Friday: Everybody Who Hates Jon Gets a Free Pontiac!

A talk show could also be problematic for Kate because she has a vexing habit of making up questions and answering them herself and calling that conversation:

"Did I feel angered and betrayed by Jon's selfishness? You bet I did."

"Do I want dressing on the side? Yes, absolutely I do."

"Is it completely hypocritical to kvetch about the paparazzi while courting them at the same time? You betcha!"

Octomom, your moment is now. Seize the day, you crazy-ass breed cow. And when you go into that meeting, you might want to take Caroline with you. Just saying.

11

You Know You Want It:
Snuggie's Embrace Will Melt You

Here in the South, we don't really do cold. Cold weather is, frankly, unseemly. We have no desire to experience it and we even feel a tad dizzy and nauseous when confronted with the sight of Southerners wading through snow drifts on the nightly news, bundled in layers of clothes.

The only time Southerners like layers is when they're in the ruffled tulle of our wedding gowns (or perhaps in the sixteen-layer chocolate cakes our sainted grandmothers used to make). If we wanted snow and cold weather, we would move to someplace like Minnesota, which even native son Garrison Keillor describes as "a state where people's tongues are routinely frozen to metal objects."

Here in the middle of the coldest winter I can remember,

the weather announcer has said that today's high will be seventeen. I want my mommy.

The only thing that's funny about this weather in our South is that it brings out the braggart in all the many thousands of Yankees who have moved here.

Oh, how they chuckle at our quaint complaints. The ruder ones are openly disdainful of our pouty reactions to this late unpleasantness.

"You call this cold?" one said to me. "Ha! When we lived in Buffalo, winters were so cold the flashers would stop women and show them a *picture* of themselves naked."

Yes, well, yok, yok, yok. All I know is, this morning, the weatherman said those two words that are like kryptonite to a Southerner: "Black ice."

The very name conjures images of church vans overturned on interstates, and sends shivers down our already shivered spines.

Here is a typical conversation between a Southern mama and her Southern daughter in the event of a prediction of the dreaded black ice from the TV weatherman:

Mama: "You can't go out tonight. John Bob on Channel 7 says it's going to be real bad out there."

Daughter: "Oh, Mama, you're so silly. I'm going out tonight and you can't stop me. Now stop worrying!"

Mama (*smiling slightly*): "He said there would be . . . *black ice* on the highways."

Daughter: "What y'all wanna watch on TV tonight?"

Northerners are unconcerned about black ice or anything else. To hear them tell it, our new Yankee-transplant neighbors never took their babies out in strollers. They simply balanced them on their feet, *March of the Penguins*-style, and went about their errands.

There was no mistaking the braggy tone of a transplant who moved here from North Dakota. He put his dog outside for a few minutes so it could do its business one night and it froze to death in mid poop.

"Yah, sure, it froze to death right dere, you betcha."

Keeping all this in mind, you can just imagine the reaction of these newcomers when our local public schools delayed opening a couple of hours "on account of it being real cold." Yep, that's what they said in just those words.

I didn't see anything funny about that. It seemed like a perfectly acceptable reaction to me. We Southerners aren't built to endure cold. We are gentle creatures that look best in sundresses and skin that is dewy with humidity. I will never again complain about a brutal August heat. This morning, it was fifty-nine degrees in my living room and I made coffee while wearing gloves.

There's nothing wrong with my heating system. It's just, like the rest of us, utterly depressed by such ridiculous expectations. Our hands, feet, and faces are chapped, rough, and red. We are sleeping in, may God have mercy on our Southern souls, sweat pants.

Meanwhile, as far south as Orlando, there were reports

of snow flurries. At Disney World, it was rumored that even Winnie the Pooh was finally contemplating putting on some pants, surely a sign of the end times.

There is one thing good to have come out of this awful cold snap we've experienced: The Snuggie.

When I opened the birthday gift from my mother-in-law a few months earlier, I had let loose with a snobby little chuckle. That was back in September when we were enjoying our normal 98 percent humidity. Good times.

"Wow," I said when I opened the box. Didn't see that one coming. A Snuggie. As seen on TV. My mother-in-law gave me a blanket with sleeves. I fretted that she was afraid I'd gained so much weight that I wouldn't be able to wear anything else, but she swore that wasn't so.

Still, a Snuggie just seemed so, I don't know, mediocre. What was I supposed to do? Wear it as I trudged through the sycamore leaves to the mailbox to see if my Cash 4 Gold check had arrived yet?

The Snuggie, like the ShamWow, was just such an infomercial hoot. You could combine the two and really have something, I told my m-i-l, a tad ungraciously, now that I think about it.

"Why not make a Snuggie entirely out of ShamWows, put it on, hose yourself down and then roll around the floor, cleaning as you go."

"Try it on," said my mother-in-law.

Great. If I opened it, there would be no way I could return it

"Good idea!" I said, with way more enthusiasm than I felt.

The box was sealed up with tape so I had to use scissors to get it open. When I finally succeeded, the Snuggie immediately expanded like a life raft, filling my mother-in-law's den and threatening to knock duh-hubby's portrait off the wall, along with the collection of candles flickering below.

Not sure why that irritates my sisters-in-law so much.

"Wow!" I said. If this thing didn't work as a cozy cover-up, it would make a fabulous drop cloth for, uh, Switzerland.

Because of its enormousness, it took me a few seconds to locate the Snuggie's actual sleeves. I haven't been this kerflummoxed by an article of clothing since I bought my first thong. Also my last, since you ask.

While the whole family watched, I put the Snuggie on as best I could and figured I'd just model it quickly and give everybody a good laugh.

Except that's not how it went.

Snuggie had me in its warm embrace. It was like those "rebirth" blankets you hear about people using to recreate the womb experience, except without all the gooey placenta crap.

No! It was nothing like that. The Snuggie wasn't some crackpot psychology experiment; it was the real deal. I never wanted to take it off. I would wear my Snuggie everywhere

I went, conducting my daily errands—bank, grocery store, post office, driving by the gym—all while wrapped, nay, swaddled in this marvelous monklike monstrosity.

I take back every hateful thing I ever said, thought, or wrote about the Snuggie. Because, the truth is, there's nothing worse than criticizing something you've never even tried. (I'm remembering *you*, deep-fried Oreos.)

Now that we're freezing every day, the Snuggie has changed my life, forcing me to feel adrift and helpless for forty minutes every week as I wait for it to finally emerge from the dryer. Lucky dryer.

So look elsewhere if you want to deride the Snuggie or mock its cheesy advertising campaign. The Snuggie is a gift from God. OK, actually Walgreens, but still.

Snuggie has sustained me through this coldest of winters. I even bought one for Duh and the Princess so the three of us could sit around the fireplace decked out in our fleecy companions. For our Christmas card this year, we even posed in front of the tree in our matching Snuggies.

Oh, I know what you're thinking . . . why not just put your robe on backwards you idiot? And you shouldn't call me an idiot by the way. What can I say? It's just not the same. The Snuggie knows what it's doing. All hail the Snuggie. And what it's doing is suffocating you with softness and warmth. Why do you think people wear them to ball games? What? They don't do that? It's just something the infomercial says?

Whatever. The Snuggie has made this wretched cold weather

almost bearable. And for that I will endure your ceaseless jokes about monasteries and cults and all the rest of it.

I will read your belittling comments while using the adorable book light that came free with the Snuggie, along with the warm sock-booties that also came with.

Wearing the Snuggie is the only thing that has helped me survive this brutal Donner party–style winter. As a matter of fact, if the Donner party had had Snuggies, they might not have turned on one another in such dramatic and distasteful fashion. Oh, they would've been hungry, all right. But they would've been warm. And given the choice, this belle chooses warmth.

12

Happy 50th Birthday, Barbie!
Midge Has Your Back (Stabbed)

Barbie and I are the same age, give or take a couple of years, so I've always felt that we were kind of like soul sistahs.

Granted, she's pretty and vapid and I'm just vapid, but we do share a love for our convertibles, and a certain bottle-blonde bond.

People who aren't as beautiful or popular as Barbie, not to name names but *Midge*, have always bad-mouthed her. It's just that ol' green-eyed monster, if you ask me. Frankly, Barbie and I are used to that stuff.

You'd think that now that Barbie is fifty, all that animosity would settle down a bit. But then I stumble across this letter written by that jealous Midge to Barbie on the occasion of her fiftieth birthday and I realize that things are worse than ever. . . .

Dear Barbie,

OMG! I can't believe you're the big 5-0! One minute you're pursuing your many fascinating careers and
patiently ignoring snippy comments about your fabulous figure, and the next minute there you are, spending another Sadday night with Ken, watching wrasslin'
on TV and drinking that new Budweiser with the
lime already in it. So highfalutin' and just like the two
of y'all to choose the fancy beer. Don't think I ever
forgot how snotty you were when I offered you some
Jeno's Pizza Rolls when you were visiting my less-
than-Dream House. You and Ken can eat that rolled-
up bait you like so much on your own time.

Oh, Barbie, I didn't mean to go off on a rant.
That's not the purpose of my greeting. I just wanted to
say, as your lifelong friend, the one with the also-ran
spouse, Alan, I, Midge, just want to say, "Welcome to
my world!" Have you seen the parody of you as Cougar
Barbie on YouTube? What do you mean, what is You-
Tube? Girrrrrl, you have gotta get out more. Things
have changed a lot since you came along in '59.

I have to admit, every time I heard some little shit
pout on Christmas morning because Santa brought me
or Skipper or Christie instead of YOU, wonderful
YOU, it did chafe a bit. OK, more than a bit. I swear
there was a time back in the mid-'70s when I toyed
with asking G.I. Joe (who, incidentally, like my Alan,

prefers a real woman with red hair, freckles, and a wardrobe of dowdy floral shifts) to, well, accidentally on purpose toss a grenade into your Dream House or at least tamper with the brakes on that ridiculous Pepto-Bismol convertible of yours.

Oh, don't look so surprised. You made life insufferable for the rest of us with your perfect proportions. Remember how you'd be wearing your black tulle "Nightclub Singer" evening gown and I'd be wearing, let's see, oh, yes, I remember now, PLAID CU-LOTTES. And who names their clothes anyway? You think I fling open my closet door (which is bifold and never works right 'cause that's all we're allowed to have here in the trailer-home park) and say, "Oh, I think I'll wear my 'Singing in the Shower' today or maybe my 'Dreamy Delight' or my 'Gold 'n' Glamour'?" Oh hell to the no. I'm lucky if I can find something that doesn't have spit-up from the grandbaby all over it. And, since you ask, he is, in fact, a bastard. Oh, I can just see your nose crawl right up your face when I say that.

But here's the thing: I don't care what you think. You're too old to threaten me and mine anymore. I'm glad we've got lil Deavis Ray the bastard in our lives now. He's just turned 3 and me and Alan have been trying to potty train him. Funny story about that: See, Deavis Ray finally used the potty for Numero Dos, as

we like to call it because we believe it's very important that Deavis be fluent in at least 2 languages. This
was a real big deal, it being the first time and all, but I
was at the Big Lots buying some old-ass frosted flakes
and missed the whole entire thing. I haven't been this
disappointed since Alan lost our Lynyrd Skynyrd Trib-
ute Band tickets in a poker game. But my Alan came
up with a solution and he sent me a picture to my
phone—not of Deavis Ray on the little plastic potty
like most people, no. He sent me a picture of the damn
poo sitting in the potty by itself. Men just don't pay
much attention to presentation sometimes.

Of course, Ken would've known better than to do
that. I know you're thinking that. But then, Ken always
was "artistic" wasn't he? And by artistic, I mean he was
gay as a circus tent in a field of flowers. Just saying.

So you're 50 now and not even a grandmama like
me. The way me and Alan see it, it's time to finally
just tell you the truth. Which, unlike your Malibu-tan
face, is going to be completely unvarnished. Here goes:
Girl, we all hated you. Even Becky, the one in the
wheelchair. In fact, she hated you the most. Hahahaha-
hahahahaha! There. I feel so much better already. The
free shrink down at the welfare office told me that I
should save myself another stroke by confronting problems (you) and not just stewing in my own juices. She's
a pretty good shrink, although I don't think she's good

with money because Alan says she's down at the Internet sweepstakes café almost as often as he is! Oh, shut up! Alan's gonna win that Pot O' Gold one day, just watch.

Oh, Barbie, now that you're 50, maybe you'll finally understand that it's inner beauty that counts. YOU SHALLOW COW! Oops. Did I just write that out loud?

Barbie, they say living well is the best revenge, and I must tell you that Alan and I have a full and productive life that has nothing to do with you but has a great deal to do with cooking up large quantities of methamphetamine in our RV and getting the young'uns to sell it to their school friends. OH, DON'T JUDGE ME! You don't know what it's been like for me living in your 38-22-34 shadow all these decades. But no more! You're just a few short years away from senior coffee at McDonald's.

The playing field is a little more even now that we're both "on in years," right, Toots?

You were always so high and mighty but now you're just old and high and mighty. Don't think I don't remember how you snickered when I told you that me and Alan spent $2,000 on that pageant dress for our baby daughter, Alan-ia. Let me tell you, we were the proudest parents in the entire Ramada Inn Conference Center when she won "Best Manicure" and got that big-ass trophy. She beat a whole roomful of other contestants, all of 'em dipped and fluffed to the nines.

When she won, I shouted out, "Well slap my ass and call me Sally!" Oh, there went your nose again. Well, get over it. At your age, making ugly faces can lead to wrinkles. Anyway, after Alan-ia got her trophy, we all went out to eat at Ruby Tuesday. Alan had a coupon for $10 off because he thinks of every-freakin'-thing, my Alan. Alan-ia is just so much like me. We got up to go pee and the waitress came along about the time we both stood up to walk to the bathroom and we said, IN UNISON, "Don't be touchin' my shit while I'm gone."

No way could I have been more proud than I was at that particular moment. We hate somebody touchin' our shit. And since we'd said it together, we had to say "Jinx!" real quick to get rid of the curse. We may not be wealthy but we're also superstitious.

Barbie, I guess all this has turned into more of an update on my full life instead of the Happy Birthday note that I had started out to write and for that, I'm sorry.

It's kinda like when we visit Alan's crazy-ass aunt, Sudie, and she just talks and talks and talks about everything in her stupid life and then, when she finally shuts up and takes a breath, you know what she says? "Well, here I go just talkin' about myself all this time. What would YOU like to know about me?"

I will close now because Alan's outside trying to show Deavis Ray how he can set his ass hairs on fire using a can of Suave Extra Hold and a torch. Again.

So, from all of your "friends" (OK, just me and Becky) at Mattel, happy damn birthday. I hope you can still fit into your "Barbie in Switzerland" ensemble because alls I got to add to this is "Yodel-lay-ye-HO!"

Gotta go now! Alan says it's past time for my "crazy pills." See what good care he takes of me?

Love,

Midge

Postscript

Aside from Barbie turning fifty, there's more exciting news this year from Mattel, which also owns the American Girl dolls. You know the ones: They're about a hundred bucks each and wear those Mennonites-in-the-airport outfits.

So what? So this. There's a new American doll named Gwen and she's *homeless*.

I'm picturing a pretty fiery board meeting as Mattel tried to figure out how to accessorize the homeless Gwen. American Girl dolls tend to have pricey accessories (who can forget the $65 plastic horse?), so how do you brand a homeless doll without seeming, well, tacky?

It's not like Mattel can, in good corporate conscience, sell a battered '86 Taurus station wagon for Gwen and her mama to sleep in.

What's next, I wonder. Mackenzie, a spunky American Girl doll who experiments with drugs and alcohol to escape the reality of her daily doings with her pervy rock-star dad?

I don't want to say Mattel is being insensitive to the plight of the homeless, although there's a definite let-them-eat-cake vibe here. On the other hand, it's not terrible to introduce your precious Oilily-clad cherub to the notion that Poor People Aren't Bad People. Except maybe for Midge.

13

Charlie Bit Your Finger? Good

'm not the only one who has noticed the depressing American obsession with all things "cute" lately. An article in *Vanity Fair* magazine confirmed something that I've suspected for a while now: We're on cute overload and it's only getting worse.

The whys could be debated. Maybe it's just an overcorrection to national angst about the economy, wars, and a health care system that is so whacked out it will pay for his fake boner pills but not for her birth control.

If you think about it long enough, you'll go crazier than a cat trying to cover shit on a marble floor. So you retreat from adult worries and sink into the soft cocoon of cute. Yes, we crave cute. Oooey, gooey cute. And while I think that's groovy for hawking kids' products, when cute is used to sell adult stuff, I find it sort of gagsome.

Do you really want to buy car insurance from a company that uses a cute little cartoon character made of money as its spokesman? I mean, this is insurance, the stuff that pays to have you and your car put back together after some asshole pulls out in front of you in his limp lil hybrid and you end up in the hospital.

And speaking of hospitals, did you know that some of them now give teddy bears and other stuffed animals to adult patients who complain about the service?

Patient: "You amputated the wrong leg, you idiot son of a whore!"

Hospital staffer: "I know! And we're really sorry. And to show how sorry we are, here's a cuddly-wuddly Mr. Snuggles the Bear for you to keep!"

Patient: "Snuggles the Bear? You think a stuffed bear that any idiot could win at the carnival by tossing plastic rings onto milk bottles is going to make up for my missing leg? *Do you???* Well, aw hell, he is kinda cute. OK. C'mere you little cutie patootie!"

God save us all.

The cute conspiracy is everywhere. How brain-dead must adults be to tolerate a commercial in which a dancing scrub mop croons ballads to its ditzy human in hopes that she'll decide to use it again for her cleaning needs?

"Martha, come quick! That mop is pretending to sing *Love Hurts* again. God that really makes me want to tell you to go scrub the kitchen floor."

And since kids aren't in charge of buying the toilet paper in most households, it's a mystery why cartoon bears with toilet paper stuck to their asses are causing formerly mature, responsible grownups to go to the grocery store and ask for help finding "the cute toilet paper that, you know, sticks to the baby bear's ass on TV."

There's a credit-card commercial where every image "smiles" at you through its shape if you look at it hard enough. Duh-hubby loves this commercial. He sits mesmerized by it, giggling at its cleverness.

"Get it? Every object is a smile. Like that car with the headlights and the grille? If you look close, it's like the car is actually smiling at you!"

Precious Lord, where is the whip-smart man I married two decades ago? The one who once gave me a card with kittens romping in a flower-covered meadow on it with the message, "Dreams don't come true"? I still laugh my ass off when I look at it. Where is the man who thought my ASK ME ABOUT MY EXPLOSIVE DIARRHEA T-shirt was as funny as I did?

Vanity Fair concluded that, "The move toward cuteness has come about partly because the idea of 'edge' has gotten old." Apparently, and it grieves me to write this, Americans are tired of cynicism, sarcasm, and all the other isms and asms that basically keep me employed.

I don't do cute. Edge I like. Cars with flower-shaped tail lights being driven by women old enough to know better? Not so much.

And get this: While I was pondering this horrifying pop-culture development, no fewer than three impossibly cute e-mails landed in my inbox. Which, by the way, I imagine to be a dark, cavelike place that smells of stale puns and bean dip. You know, the kind of place where there's a stained VOTE FOR PEDRO T-shirt wadded up on the floor in the corner.

Two of these e-mails were accompanied by smiley flower "emoticons" that made me lightheaded with all their winking and tomfoolery. Which is the word of a curmudgeon, now that I think about it. An edgy curmudgeon. I don't know how to make the winky face or the frown face or any of the despicable acts that grown adults force their punctuation keys to perform. Every morning when I check my e-mail, I must first be assaulted by a screen-sized emoticon before the mail is loaded. WTF? One has a lower case *d* and a lowercase *b* with the message "Listening to Music!" Another uses *m*'s and *o*'s to create a "Monkeyface!" Are you serious?

This morning's e-mail included a dozen criminally cute photos of kittens sleeping on computers and curled up inside their own food bowls, as well as one of a baby asleep, face-down, inside his daddy's large, and I'm guessing stinky, running shoe. The last photo was of a huge orange tabby cat asleep in a lasagna dish accompanied by a caption that asked earnestly "Have you ever been this tired?"

Tired enough to crawl into a Pyrex casserole dish or somebody's nasty-behind shoe? Can't say as I have. But my friend

Lisa will crawl into a Laundromat dryer if you buy her enough beer. What? Not cute enough?

Over on Facebook, one of my "friends" asked if I would please accept his gift of "one wet puppy nose!" To which all I can muster in reply is a world-weary, "Dude."

Facebook is downright obsessed with cute, between its imaginary farm-building games and, just today, the insistence that we use our baby pictures as profile pictures. Sorry. It's creepy seeing your boss naked in a kitchen sink circa 1958. And I don't want to type in what color bra I'm wearing in my status update (but don't tell the guys 'cause it's fun to keep 'em guessing! Smiley face, smiley face, winking emoticon). What is this? Sixth grade?

But back to this crazy-ass notion that people are tired of edgy. This is scarier to me than a roomful of yard-sale Beanie Babies. This ghastly culture of cuteness, a massive group hug, if you will, could kill my career. And I believe we can all agree that this would signal the end of civilization as we know it because, in the immortal words of anchorman Ron Burgundy, "I'm kind of a big deal."

OK, maybe not. But I do so love the snarky, the sneering, and the snotty. There's simply no room for all these YouTube videos of laughing babies that you people keep forwarding to me. That little kid who squawks about how "Chah-wee bit my finger again"? Not funny. Ditto the little boy who's still loopy from his trip to the dentist, which was sent to me by a friend who said, "This is the funniest thing I've ever seen!"

Yep. Nothing says hilarious like videotaping your kid while he's recovering from oral surgery. Maybe he can return the favor one day after your hemorrhoid operation. Payback's a bitch, eh?

Clearly she has never seen Bon Qui Qui at Burger King. Now that's some funny shit; Google it.

The cuteness craze is even taking over food. Cupcakes weren't cute enough. Now there are miniature cupcakes topped with fluffy-wuffy icing and teeny-tiny décor-wations. Even the traditional wedding cake is being replaced by cupcake towers. Sure, they're tasty enough, but you can't really jam a cupcake into your spouse's face in that weirdly aggressive reception ritual. For that, you need a giant, very un-cute wedge of cake. You want him to be picking red velvet crumbs out of his nose hairs for weeks. You can't do that with a cupcake.

Of course I'm looking to blame somebody for all this and I have decided the whole thing is the fault of, you guessed it, the Japanese. Ever since they invented Hello Kitty, the world hasn't been the same. You can safely chart the rise of The Culture of Cute ever since that flat-faced skank started showing up everywhere.

The first time I saw Hello Kitty was on a tour boat that was circling the Statue of Liberty. For some reason, I was the only non-Japanese person on the entire boat. And every single occupant of the boat, even the *men*, were wearing some article of clothing—purse, shirt, jewelry—with that mutant white head on it. Creepy thing doesn't even have a mouth. How do you get such a fat head if you can't even eat? OK, I've overthinking it.

Stop the madness. Embrace the snark. Or, yes, I will come to your house, kill your puppies, and kick in the door of that stupid Lego car you drive that you insist is "so ugly it's cute!"

News flash: It really is just ugly. What? That hurt your feelings? Oh, no! I'm sooooo sah-wee. Here, have a minicupcake and Mr. Snuggles the Bear to make it all better. Asshat.

14

Chinese Bachelors Would Be
Lucky to Find Cougar

You remember that whole one-child limit thing in China? Seemed like a good idea at the time now, didn't it? When your population hovers around 1.3 billion and you're not quite as large as the United States, landwise, you've got to do something.

So you set limits and enforce them. One child per family. What could possibly go wrong?

Well, funny you should ask.

According to the Chinese Academy of Social Sciences (motto: "Everybody Wang Chung tonight"), in about ten years, there will be approximately twenty-four million Chinese men who won't be able to find a wife. That's right; not even an ugly one.

But wait, that's not all! In a cruel little quirk of demographics, at the exact same time, China's elderly population will explode. What does it all mean? That's easy. Ten years from now, the typical Chinese household will consist of an elderly couple whose bachelor sons are getting older and crankier and less-laid by the minute. Doesn't that sound dreamy?

Let's face it. It's hardly a harmonious situation, this clash of the generations. Even ten years from now, it's possible that those very sons will still have to spend the better part of an hour trying to explain to their aged parents that most people have voice mail, not answering machines.

Which means that you end up burying your head in your hands while your mama shrieks into the phone to your cousin: "Pick up Ming Sai, it's me! Pick up! I know you're there! Your auntie said you were home! (*very long pause*) If you there, why you not answer the phone? You know it's me! OK, I guess you're not there after all. Call me!"

You can try to explain voice mail a million times but it will never matter to the elderly parent, Chinese or not. They still think it's an answering machine and you're just sitting there ignoring them.

This could go on, literally, for hours.

All of which is to say that it's never a good idea for grown sons to move back in with the 'rents no matter where you live. In America, almost everybody knows an old couple or two whose shaggy-ass son lives in the basement eating Fritos and drinking bong water, and it only makes for a miserable family dynamic.

Just call me Dr. Phil-lis.

And how's that workin' for ya?

Being something of a Chinese-history scholar myself—I have watched *Mulan* at least forty-eight times, learning to love it even after discovering that *Donny Osmond* was the voice behind the fiercest warrior in China—I feel uniquely qualified to say that this is a recipe for generational disaster.

The frustrated parents won't even be able to nag their sons around the breakfast table—"Why you don't date that nice Kai-ying?"—because Kai-ying will be able to pick and choose from hundreds, perhaps thousands, of aspiring suitors. For a country that hasn't exactly been supportive of women achieving greatness, or, hell, even supportive of them being born in the first place, this is revenge as sweet as the sticky rice pudding at Ting Ting's mile-long buffet, no lie.

I hope my Chinese sistahs are enjoying this attention a little bit. After all, every desperate male suitor will need to bring his "A" game to the courting ritual if he wants to have any slim chance of attracting a wife. That means he can forget about showing up at Chen-chi's house in some triflin' rickshaw of a car and expecting her parents to fawn all over him with tea and crumpets and shit.

Chen-chi's holding all the cards now and she likey.

Since the Chinese people, if *Mulan* is the historical

document I accept it to be, are obsessed with matchmaking, it would appear that, at last, the shoe is on the other tightly bound foot, eh?

Now, it's the male clients who must seek out a matchmaker or, if that's too low-tech, there's always eHarmony or Match.com, though I expect those sites to crash from the sheer volume of desperate Chinese bachelors. Moonlit walks on the beach? Don't make me laugh. I repeat: "A" game.

This wretched gender imbalance, some social scientists predict, will result in a surge of marriages between young men and much older women. These most honorable *cougar* will be too old to have children which is your basic win-win sitchy-ation.

But what of those who really want to have kids?

Assuming the Chinese man won't want to cheat and get himself a mail-order bride from another country, how should he go about making himself stand out from all the rest?

I'm thinking he could take a page or two from Barack Obama's playbook. Love him or hate him, the dude knows how to treat a lady.

Let's face it: Husbands and boyfriends across this great nation are whining because Obama is making their date nights look lame. This was sooooo not a problem during the Bush years. Remember when W's idea of a romantic getaway was to fire up Air Force One and fly to Crawford, Texas, for a weekend of brush clearing and faux cattle roping? We never heard what poor Laura Bush did during those less-than-sumptuous vacays but I'm imagining it involved cooking stew for the boys in the bunkhouse and reading some bodice rippers to while away those hot, dull afternoons.

Never once in those eight years did I nudge Duh in the ribs and demand a date night like poor Laura Bush was being treated to.

Even Bill Clinton wasn't known for putting together an awesome date night. At least not with Hillary, bless her heart.

No, Clinton took virtually no time away from Washington, let alone whisking his bride to a Broadway show and dinner in New York like Obama did. Just because.

When he needed to go to Paris for some summit thing or the other, do you think Obama told Michelle to watch the kids and he'd bring her back one of those Eiffel Towers with the thermometer inside it?

Hell, no! He took her along and even carved out a date night of foie gras and pheasant de truffled snootypants right beneath that famous thermometer tower.

See, Chinese suitors? This is how it's done. Your dates will have to have some serious "Wow!" factor. Otherwise, and I really can't state this strongly enough, you're going to be in charge of the prune juice acquisition for a long time to come, just saying.

To be honest, the Obamas' European adventure made me a little pouty because, like a lot of American women, the closest I've come to an exotic European vacation is ordering the "Tour of Italy" trio of I-talian favorites at the Olive Garden recently.

And since you ask, yes, it was pretty damn tasty.

Chinese men, listen the hell up! I know what I'm talking about when I tell you that Obama is The Man when it comes to planning date nights.

Even on a night when he was going to an NBA playoff game with the boys, he made sure to have an early date with his wife, at Citronelle, an uber-ritzy restaurant in Georgetown.

Do *not* follow the example of poor duh-hubby when it comes to a date night. When I complained that he never took me anywhere unless I suggested it first, Duh ran out of the room and returned a few minutes later holding aloft a raggedy coupon he'd found in the newspaper for two-for-one dinners at Ruby Tuesday.

Anticipating that I would squeal with glee at this, Duh held up his hand as if to stop the celebrating that hadn't actually happened in the first place.

"You can't use it for the premium steaks and you have to eat the broccoli instead of the salad bar," he said.

"But broccoli gives me gas," I said, regretting it instantly. If I want to be treated like Michelle Obama and taken to tony restaurants all over the world, I can't go around talking like that. "I mean, er, flatulence."

Of course, Chinese men, your girlfriend can make pooty noises with her armpits in front of your whole family and y'all can't complain because, as the social scientists have said, there just won't be enough women to go around. You'll just have to suck it up if she's weird, demanding, and wants to bring her fire-breathing dragon of a mama to live with y'all.

Don't even think about complaining when they both ask you to cut their toenails. It's the least you can do.

Don't be cheap about the wedding either. Here in the American South, we all know that only heathens and Yankees get married at hotels. Just remember that when it comes time to pick the spot. Don't complain about how much it's going to cost because Hop Sing is right around the corner waiting to pounce.

A final bit of politico-inspired advice: In general, when it comes to women, if South Carolina governor Mark Sanford did it, you don't. This is an excellent guideline, regardless of country of origin.

While Sanford was highly hateable for his insistence on asking his wife's blessing for his affair with the Argentinean hoochie-mama, it wasn't until I read Jenny Sanford's tell-most book that I realized what a turd he really was. Is. Turns out he once asked his wife to give back the diamond necklace he'd given her for Christmas because he decided it was too expensive and he wanted to take it back and get the money.

Be generous, Chinese grooms-to-be. Before your lotus flower can even mention something she'd like, anticipate it and present it to her.

The world is her oyster now, big boy. Don't blow it unless you and your brothers want to be sitting at your mama's kitchen table clipping those Poligrip coupons out of the Sunday paper for a very, very long time to come. Think about it.

15

Crappy Science Fair Didn't Even
Have Any Rides

After six years of science fair projects, the Princess had never advanced beyond competition in her own school. Not because her projects hadn't been exceptionally innovative, impeccably researched, and masterfully displayed, but rather because the judges were idiots.

Hey, I call 'em as I see 'em.

But this year would be different. This year, the Princess collaborated with a friend on an awesome project that involved building an incubator to grow germs and then proving that, yes, double-dipping chips and dips does transfer bacteria from one person to another. They even had a clever title: "The George Costanza Project," named after the *Seinfeld* episode in which George gets in trouble for double-dipping at a party.

My participation in this project was limited, as always, to driving to Staples and buying the trifold display board. I'm all about the science. As long as it isn't too science-y, you know.

The project turned out great (but then, they always did, year after year, see "idiots" above). But this year, something wonderful happened: The project was selected to compete at the county level!

OK, here's the thing: I've never been to a countywide science fair before. I mean, who goes to those things unless their kid is competing, right? Other than those wacky homeschoolers who like to go so they can snicker behind their hands at the pitiful public school kids' ideas of advanced science.

This countywide fair was, I have to say, quite an eye-opener. Turns out this is really kind of a big deal. To the parents. You've heard the term "helicopter parents" I'm sure. The trendy way to describe the current culture of parents overseeing everything even their adult children do? Well, these were more like Sikorsky Super Stallion helicopter parents.

Me? Not so much. I dumped the girls in the gym and immediately went in search of the $3 pizza slice I'd seen advertised out front.

I bought a slice and stood around observing some of the other parents. Who all seemed to know each other really well. The only thing missing was the secret handshake. There was a lot of "Hey! Great to see you again'!" but I had the feeling they probably kinda hated each other a little. There were clenched teeth, through which they would say things like, "Ohhhh, I hear that the judges are hoping for something along the lines of optimizing turbine blade efficiency by manipulating boundary layer separation but that's sooooooo 2009 in my opinion. What's your Andy Jr. doing?"

And this would be followed by discussions about winning projects of the past. Things like "national organics control aggregation of mercury sulfide nanoparticles in freshwater systems" and "functional genomic frameworks for chemotherapeutic drug improvement and identification."

OK, dipping a potato chip into some onion dip and then doing it again was starting to look pretty damn lame at this point.

I wanted to join in all the "fun science talk" but was clearly out of my league. These parents were battle-scarred veterans of some weird science wars I'd never known anything about. Until that damn potato chip landed me here and away from my planned normal evening of eating said chips and watching E! TV live from Sundance, where Jon Gosselin has now stepped into the role of "pudgy asshole who shows up everywhere pretending to be actually famous" that was occupied at one time by Kato Kaelin.

Standing in the hallway, alone with my pizza, it was obvious that this was a middle-school clique of an entirely different kind. These parents were pretty damn smart with all their talk of genomes and cantilevering.

I'm not for one minute implying that the kids don't do all their own work on these science fair projects. No, I'm just coming right out and saying it.

After a half hour or so, the judges walked toward the gym doors and there was a somewhat hysterical plea over the PA: *"All parents must exit the gym, repeat, must exit the gym, in order for the judging to begin."*

A couple of the moms looked as if they might have to be Tasered to get out of there as they fluffed with final details at their kid's display area. Almost every single kid with one of those hovering parents sat in a folding chair in front of his project, head buried in a book, oblivious to the fact that, apparently, his future, and perhaps the future of the entire free world, was on the line.

Finally, the fifteen or so judges filed into the gym, all wearing white lab coats and holding clipboards.

"Look! It's a nerd parade!" I squealed to the mom standing next to me. She walked away. If I'd been a science fair experiment, the title would've been called "Corrosive Relationships."

The truth was, I wasn't used to the rarified air of the advanced competition and it showed. The in-school contests were more laid back because almost nobody really expected to win. That's how you end up with my all-time favorite: "Meth: Friend or Foe," beautifully displayed for all the world and, most likely, Child Protective Services, to see.

The judging was followed by an open house and assembly

for the awards ceremony. By this time, duh-hubby had gotten off work and was able to join me and several hundred other parents in the auditorium. I'd seen the competition during a walk-through in the gym and was fairly certain that unless the Princess had cobbled together an atom splitter in the past ninety minutes, she was, I believe the scientific term is: "toast." I consoled myself with the knowledge that I'd TiVo-d Jon Gosselin at Sundance so the night really wasn't a total loss.

A very serious and sincere woman who looked a lot like Ms. Frizzle in *The Magic School Bus* books told us that she was in charge of this rodeo and there was much applause. A few of the parents stood up and applauded. *"Suck ups"* I said-coughed into my hand. Her assistant stood like Vanna White, repeatedly motioning to a table full of trophies in varying sizes.

Trophies that we damn sure wouldn't be taking home.

The couple beside us, fortunately, were also first-timers.

"There's some weird shit goin' on up in here," the man said. I nodded in agreement.

Winners were announced in elementary, middle, and high school divisions, plus some kids won special trophies donated by local industries. One little girl, about eight years old, won four different trophies. Her parents squealed and did high fives. Every time. The couple beside me looked down at their daughter who was, at this point, sobbing into her best Sunday dress, having realized that she'd lost the elementary round.

"Take her for ice cream," I told my new friend.

"Only if I can get beer, too," he said grimly.

It's true, I thought to myself. All the good ones really *are* taken.

On the way out, there was some sobbing—by the parents. One parent comforted a distraught mom by saying that, "It's obvious that these judges had no clue what makes a good project at state!"

"Yeah," I said. "No clue! They got no clue!"

"That's right," she said, sniffling a bit. "What was your project?"

I'm not proud of what happened next. Why couldn't I have just been honest about the project that the Princesses had worked on for the better part of four weeks, taking breaks only long enough to talk for a few hours about how awesomely ripped Taylor Lautner is.

How could I fancy up this suddenly plain-Jane science fair project? I couldn't just talk about chips and dip and then re-dipping and how it's all icky and germy.

"Oh, my daughter and her friend tested the, uh, molecular structure, of the, uh, bacterium posterity of the random accelerated protein inhibitor, uh, rubric."

I've discovered that if you put "rubric" in any conversation, you automatically sound smarter. Try it.

While I thought that sounded pretty good for something on the fly, it was obvious that I was faking it. The woman nodded quickly, then skittered down the hall where she was comforted with a big hug from the mom of a little boy who had built a hand-blown glass harmonica and PowerPointed a presentation demonstrating how well he could play Canon in D on it. I knew the boy and knew that he had done every single bit of the work by himself. And he hadn't won. See idiot judges above.

As predicted, this would be the end of the line for our little family. Clutching the trifold board and accompanying handouts, we walked out of the auditorium and into the freezing February night. There was no time for regrets. The truth is, we lost to a kid whose project title made us look at each other and say, "Do whaaaaat?" The little shit clearly deserved to win and advance to district, possibly even state, nation, and Interplanetary King of the Universe science fair.

Wrapping my arm around her shoulders, I looked the Princess in the eye.

She looked a little down, I thought.

"Don't worry, honey," I said. "We'll get 'em next year!"

"No we won't," she said.

"Yeah, I know."

16

What's Farsi for "Stay Outta My Love Life"?

As a churchgoing woman, I'm getting more than a little tired of hearing about all these pastors who are instructing their congregations to, well, do it. And do it a lot.

As we Southern Methodists like to say, "Settle down, Reverend, you've done gone from preachin' into meddlin'.

It's a trend, hons, and I'm here to tell you that it's scarier than the words "First Dude Todd Palin." Nah, I'm kidding. Nothing's scarier than that. (Except, perhaps, that I just this morning learned that pumpernickel, which I love, is literally translated to mean "goblin who breaks wind." Scary, right?)

But getting back to bidness, the Associated Press reports that ministers in Kansas, Florida, and Texas have asked, nay, instructed, ordained, and decreed, that their married congregants make hot monkey love for up to thirty days in a row.

Now I totally get that you'd do that in Kansas, because once basketball season winds down, really, what else is there to do? Take your time answering that; I'll wait. Still waiting. But Florida? Did they shut down Disney and nobody told me?

In Texas, the Reverend Ed Young has challenged couples in his Dallas church to have seven straight days of sex. Upon hearing this, a Tampa minister said he'd recommend thirty straight days of sex. Big D, indeed. I'm guessing Rev. Young will up the ante to "Every married couple will have sex every day for ten years period, so *nanny nanny boo boo, stick your head in doo doo.*"

And while I like a little healthy competition in most things, this seems more than a tad intrusive. Here's how I look at it: At my church, we recently had a contest between all the Sunday school classes to see which class could bring in the most cans of soup for the local food pantry. Bottom line: I don't think the homeless give a happy damn if a bunch of Methodists they don't even know personally are feet-to-Jesus thirty days a month just because the preacher says we should be, but I'm pretty sure they're fired up about those twenty-four hundred cans of soup.

Pastor Bob is a fine fella in every way (except a pesky allegiance to the vile Duke Blue Devils, owing to an unfortunate stint at divinity school there), but I can tell you that if he ever stood up in the pulpit and instructed us to "get busy," I'd run outta there like my clothes were on fire.

So, yes, I'm grateful not to be in the Kansas congregation

of the Reverend Timmy Gibson, who recently asked his church members to have sex every day during the month of February. I'm guessing he selected February because it's the month of love, also groundhogs, but I'm guessing he was thinking about love.

The icky thing was he didn't call it sex. He called it "hanky-panky."

Hanky-panky?

This calls to mind the practiced faux blush of Bob Eubanks, host of the old *Newlywed Game* back in the '70s. (Quick aside: Remember the classic question when ol' Bob asked, "Gentlemen, what do you think your wife would say would be the most unusual place you've ever made whoopee?" and, sure enough, one of the more candid husbands proudly held up a card that read, "In the butt.")

Indeed.

You're probably wondering why preachers care so much about their parishioners' sex life when there are obviously so many more pressing problems that the world's spiritual leaders need to address. And by spiritual leaders, I'm not talking about that loony Pat Robertson who thinks the Haitians deserve to die in earthquakes because they sold their souls to the devil. What a tool.

The answer is simple: These ministers believe that all marriages will improve through better intimacy.

That's right. Nothing says better intimacy quite like duty sex, am I right?

Rev. Gibson defends the trend by saying that sex is a topic that should be talked about from a biblical perspective.

Verily, I say to thee, it is not. Sex is a topic that should be talked about between two consenting adults after a couple of glasses of decent grocery store wine and maybe a foot massage.

Look it up. I think it's in Ephesians somewhere.

This sort of foolishness gives religion a bad name. The same way that Mark Sanford did. (Yes, yes, I'm not ready to leave him quite yet. He is, after all, the one who said he wished he'd kept his "genie in the bottle," which was simply too delicious to resist making fun of.)

Sanford, or Dope Pius, as I like to call him, tried to put a religious spin on his affair with the Argentinean Hoochita. When he visited her in New York, they went to church and took along his spiritual advisor.

Sanford's affair, then, is somehow a spiritual, God-sanctioned tryst? To hear him tell it, it was the same old tired story that so many of us have lived: You go to Uruguay with a bunch of your congressmen friends, you decide to go clubbing, you lock eyes across the dance floor with a woman with teasing tan lines, and you spend the rest of the evening murdering the salsa as only a middle-aged white man can.

Yes, clearly, so far it's God's will. Sanford eventually took Hoochita, his announced "soul mate" (pausing to gag a little here) to church services. In his defense, Sanford did ask his wife, Jenny, to join them on this trip, but she wisely took a pass, perhaps quashing forever Sanford's hopes for a three-some and the chance to write the letter he'd always dreamed of writing: "Dear Penthouse Forum, I'm the embattled governor of a small Southern state and I never thought this would happen to me. . . ."

Religion and sex shouldn't be discussed in public, not by preachers and certainly not by lovesick Southern governors who are thinking with only one branch of government, if you get my drift.

Mingling sex and religion is bad enough, but when it's used for national security, things get really squirrely.

When the CIA realized they needed Taliban information, they came up with a plan to bribe the old warlords—whose religion encourages them to have many young wives—with Viagra.

You thought money and guns would be sufficient? That's so 2002.

For someone like me, whose knowledge of CIA covert operations comes exclusively from *Get Smart* (the old TV show *and* the movie, so it's not like I'm a complete moron), this was quite a revelation.

Sneaking little blue pills to the pooped old Afghan chieftains would've never occurred to me. If I wanted to get some Taliban intelligence, I would have, like any good daughter of the South, shown up with bribery in the form of an attractively garnished deviled egg plate or perhaps a red velvet cake.

Since the Afghan chieftains have many wives, per their

wacko religion, and some of those wives are distressingly young, the CIA decided to get in bed with, so to speak, the old warlords and give 'em something they couldn't get anywhere else.

"We wanted to keep them firmly on our side," a CIA agent said, with nary a hint of irony.

Before Viagra became the bartering tool of choice, the CIA had been using less inventive strategies, such as trading tooth extractions for Taliban supply route information. Now to you and me, who are used to getting our teeth removed in sanitary offices by men and women with many boats and homes to pay for, this doesn't seem like all that big of a deal, but you have to remember that things are a bit more primitive in Afghanistan. Their oral surgeons usually have only one boat to pay for at most.

Clearly Viagra is a lot more fun than getting your teeth yanked out of your head with implements most likely involving slammed doors and long pieces of string.

Yes, a lot more fun. Said the old Afghan chieftains after a few days of Love, American Style: "Me likey." Or something like that. Gawd, it's not like I can speak Farsi, I mean except for basic stuff like "Where is the bathroom?" or "Do y'all have a Pizza Slut up in here?" Important shit like that.

Thanks to American ingenuity, the Afghan bigwigs have a spring in their steps and the newly dissed Taliban is left scratching its collective turban and wondering what the hell went wrong with their supply routes.

Hey! Maybe this is the way to finally lure Osama out of the hills at long last. Just leave a trail of little blue pills at the mouth of his cave and he'll follow them all the way into the waiting paddy wagon.

Mission freakin' accomplished.

Of course, while some have praised the CIA's brilliant plan, no one has really spoken up for the young wives, who, bless their hearts, were probably thrilled that their husband didn't have any lead in his pencil, so to speak. Now that they have his CIA-induced groove back, the wives will be expected to service the old goats. Since many, if not all, of these young wives aren't exactly the result of a committed, caring relationship involving mutual love and respect, this introduces a major ick factor into the entire arrangement.

No matter whether it's coming from a pulpit in Kansas or a CIA operative knocking on a tent door with a gleam in his eye, mixing religious beliefs and mooney-gooney isn't good for anybody.

And, in the long run, it's even scarier than pumpernickel.

17

Give Us Your Poor, Your Tired, Your Kinda Creepy Masses

As I write this, Bernie Madoff is getting settled into his new prison-home just up the road from me here in North Carolina. I'm tempted to make him a banana pudding or something.

And by "something," I mean a layer cake made entirely of poo.

When new neighbors move to "the southern part of heaven," we generally go to great pains to make them feel welcome. Usually, we'll give them a couple of days to settle in, and then we'll show up with a butter pecan pound cake, still warm from the oven, or perhaps pimento cheese made from some long-dead aunt's secret recipe. (The secret is usually a splash of Grand Marnier, but don't tell anyone I told you.)

But Madoff's swindling of the innocent and the greedy

alike to the tune of $50 billion has left me feeling less than charitable when it comes to welcoming our new and most infamous resident. Other North Carolinians feel the same way. Truth be told, I don't think Madoff could be any more reviled if he'd shown up at Butner Federal Correctional Complex toting an oil portrait of William Tecumseh Sherman to hang on his cell wall.

Madoff isn't happy to be here in the Good Old North State, whose motto, incidentally, is *Esse Quam Videri* which might as well be "Baaaah, Ram, Ewe" for all I can remember from seventh-grade state history. But I think it had to do with being an upright soul. Which he clearly isn't.

Madoff was exiled to North Carolina despite repeated pleas to let him stay in a federal prison much closer to his Manhattan home. All y'all say "Awwwwww." What can I tell you, Bernie? Some things in life, like having to eat Fancy Feast and ramen noodles because somebody stole all your retirement savings, just aren't fair, are they?

Bright side: Your new digs near the Research Triangle Park (where we keep our smartest Yankees) are just a short ninety-minute drive down I-40 from The World's Largest Frying Pan. Not that you'll ever see it, bless your old-ass thieving heart.

Bernie, while you will never get to enjoy all that our lovely state has to offer, that's certainly not true of your wife, Ruth. Why, pray tell, isn't the missus down here scoping out a new home? May I suggest the trailer park not far from Butner? It's the one where, not that long ago, one brother fatally stabbed another over who would get the last fried pork chop on the platter.

Yep, that sounds about right.

I don't feel a lot of sympathy for Ruth Madoff except when I see those photos of her leaving the prison on visiting day and see that her roots are clearly no longer being scrupulously maintained by Enrique of Park Avenue, or whomever, for more money than the average Family Dollar store manager makes in a year.

It wasn't just me who noticed that Ruth's roots were being neglected. The *New York Times* reported that she's been barred from her favorite salon as well as booted from her gym, personal florist, and even her favorite Italian bistro. Oh, no! Not the personal florist!

Well, it's like they say: When God closes one (cell) door, he just opens up a window. (Settle down, Bernie, I'm speaking metaphorically here.) If Ruth moves down here, she can get to know the floral stylists at the Piggly Wiggly grocery store closest to Butner. There, she will find a splendid selection of posies, some even accented by spray glitter at no additional charge! We Southerners have an irrational fondness for spray glitter, even those of us who like to pretend that we're above that sort of tacky display. You have not lived 'til you've seen my great Aunt Lu-Dean's holiday table with glitter-sprayed magnolia leaves glued to clothespins for place card holders.

It's a freakin' vision.

So, yes, Ruth, the Piggly Wiggly can answer your floral needs. Sure, you might *think* you don't like blue carnations now, but they'll grow on you and, best of all, they're just 50 cents apiece with your hawg heaven discount card!

If Ruth Madoff does decide to move to North Carolina to avoid those tiring trips to visit Bernie in the pokey, she will need to weigh in, sooner or later, on that most holy of matters in this state. We don't let just anybody in here. Well, sometimes we do. John Edwards' mistress is fluffing new pillows at her beach digs not far from here, bless her fornicatin' heart.

Ruth Madoff, Reille Hunter, and anyone else who moves to North Carolina will be allowed to settle in and get their bearings a little bit before someone, eventually, asks them that most important question: Do you prefer your barbecue with the pungent vinegar-based sauce of the Eastern part of the state or do you enjoy the odious tomato-based sauce favored by everyone else? What? Ruth Madoff doesn't eat barbecue on account of being Jewish? Holy Hadassah, Batgirl! I smell deal breaker.

I have to give Ruth props for standing by her jerk-of-a-man despite constantly being photographed and scrutinized. A recent photo showed her clutching a Ziploc bag full of cash on her way out of Butner, reminding me of a scene in *The Sopranos* where it was clear that even though mobster Johnny Sack was in jail, he made sure his beloved Ginny would never be without cash.

Which is not to imply that Bernie Madoff has any ties to organized crime whatsoever. No, surely organized crime has some standards.

North Carolina seems to have had its share of the spotlight this year, but we lost out to Mississippi when it came to being host state for Tiger Woods' sexual rehab clinic.

Too bad. We were going for the trifecta of creepy new residents but Mississippi snuck in there and stole Tiger from us with its much lauded Gentle Path sex-addict program, which included, I kid you not, an obstacle course among the pine trees to "boost self-esteem."

Dude. For starters, if there's anyone who can come out of the pine trees with a win, it's Tiger. Just ask Phil Mickelson. And self-esteem? I'm thinking that is soooo not a problem for him. Yes, yes, I get the whole poor little lonesome boy inside seeking validation in all the wrong places and a bevy of unresolved issues from growing up fast and famous, but have you seen Tiger's wife? Elin Woods has managed to do the impossible: make me feel genuinely sorry for a billionaire Swedish bikini model.

So, no, I don't buy it, Sigmund Floyd. I think Tiger's got sex addiction the same way I got molten lava chocolate cake addiction. He loves it. It's awesome. It makes his thighs all dimply. Oh, sorry, maybe that was just the cake.

Tiger reportedly transformed his rehab crib to the tune of $100,000 in upgrades. (You really didn't expect him to do his "shame reduction" workshop with *those* drapes, now did you?) So this doesn't sound like a man with low self-esteem to me.

There was also buzz that when Tiger walked into a room at rehab, others were asked to leave immediately. Which must've made the whole group therapy a tad problematic.

"My name is Tiger Woods and I'm a sex addict."

Silence.

The "body count" last I heard was fifteen, but it could still go higher. There are still a few precincts out in the hinterlands waiting to be counted, and don't forget, we still haven't heard from the Broward County lunchroom ladies. He's a playa, and shame on his married self, but addiction? I don't think so.

Of course, while womanizing wrongdoers John Edwards and Tiger Woods have apologized ad nauseum for their transgressions, there's really only one way they can rehab their images. Edwards thought rebuilding houses in Haiti would do the trick, and Tiger is blathering on about his foundation do-gooding, but that sort of penance is just so very last century. No, there is clearly only one true path to redemption. I am speaking of course of *Dancing With the Stars*.

Once I saw disgraced former congressman Tom DeLay bustin' a move on the show, I realized that's the next step for the hangdog Woods and Edwards and maybe even Elliot Spitzer and (yes, once more, give it up for . . .) Mark Sanford.

Somewhere Michael Vick's agent must be slapping himself upside the head and wondering why he didn't think of pitching his client to the *DWTS* producers. (Although they'd have to make sure that when Vick puts on the dog, he doesn't really . . . well, you get the idea.)

What better way to rehab a reeking image than to put on a zoot suit and murder the Charleston in front of God and Tom Bergeron?

DeLay bragged that he lost twelve pounds to get in shape for the show. How ironic. All that weight loss and he remains completely full of shit.

Opening up *DWTS* to famous disgraced womanizers would be a mite problematic, given the sexy costumes worn by the professional partners. Tiger, ever conscious of holding on to whatever endorsements he can, would have to announce that he resists arousal thanks to frequent meditative pauses sponsored by Cymbalta.

Edwards, whose tryst with Hunter, a videographer, included rumors of a (ick) sex tape, would have to resist cutting the rug and asking, "Did you get that or do we need to go again? Cause, you know, I'm fine if we have to go again. Really? You got it? Are you sure?"

On second thought, maybe *DWTS* should stick with its traditional assortment of plucky downwardly mobile celebs who tend to get cast: Your Jane Seymours. Your Adam Carollas. Your Harry Hamlins. I kind of like seeing the cute kid from some '80s sitcom all grown up and fox-trotting in a game attempt to recapture the glory days of Urkel.

At least that would've prevented the likes of DeLay and famezilla Kate Gosselin from joining the scripted fun. It would've been *much* more gratifying to see tubby ex-hubby, Jon, doing his dance image-rehab. Can't you just see him shimmying in his little-boy tees while simultaneously smoking and leering at somebody's underage daughter in the front row? It'll be hard for Kate's partner to convince her that she doesn't get to lead. Kate has said she'll do what it takes to feed her family and, by God, if that means wearing glitzy dresses and working out with the hunk of the month, well, so be it.

She's a giver, that one.

And so am I, so I'm now going to share with y'all a recipe for that butter pecan cake I mentioned earlier. It's perfect for picnics, potlucks or, yes, even the pokey.

SUPER-EASY BUTTER-PECAN POUND CAKE

4 eggs
1 cup milk
⅔ cup vegetable oil
1 teaspoon vanilla
1 cup chopped pecans, divided
1 box butter pecan cake mix
1 can coconut-pecan frosting

Preheat oven to 350 degrees (325 for dark pans). Grease and flour a tube or Bundt pan. (Or cheat and use Baker's Joy like I do.)

Mix eggs, milk, oil, vanilla and half the pecans together.

Add cake mix and beat well. Fold the can of frosting into the cake mixture and stir until incorporated. Pour the remaining pecans into the bottom of the pan. Pour cake batter over top. Bake 1 hour (or longer, until cake springs back when you touch it).

Note: This cake is very rich and dense, so a little goes a long way. It has a from-scratch taste so people will think you went to a lot of trouble. Don't tell 'em any different.

18

Bad Economy Waste-es My Time
and Disgust-es Me

Now comes the sad(ish) news that *Reader's Digest* has declared bankruptcy, a phrase that never fails to crack me up ever since I saw Michael Scott, the wrenchingly dim boss on *The Office* walk around solemnly and loudly announcing "I declare bankruptcy!" thinking that was all there was to it.

Oh, if only.

Many teams of lawyers will be working to prop up the world's most reliable magazine-slash-coaster to make it profitable again.

I hope it works because it's powerfully depressing to think that, one day in the near future, toilet tanks across this great land will sit unadorned.

Ah, *Reader's Digest*. A magazine that earned a solid following for many decades for leaving stuff *out*.

It's puzzling in the same way that decaf often costs more than regular and sugar-free muffins are always more expensive. But when it comes to the information age, we can't get enough and maybe that's why we should've realized *Reader's Digest*'s days were numbered.

(Although, it must be said that its retelling of the moldy classics in condensed book form are awesome. Here's a synopsis of *Romeo and Juliet* RD-style: "Couple contends with bickering parents who oppose their romance; both die.")

With its comforting penchant for articles like "Seven Ways to Keep Your Bird Safer!" you have to wonder if the original article contained three other really important ways that you'll never know about.

Condensation may not be the best thing in all cases but I've got a soft spot for *Reader's Digest* ever since they paid me $100 for a joke I submitted many years ago.

I don't remember what the joke was but I remember being giddy when the check came and I could officially add "magazine contributor" to a resume that, at the time, had "fry cook" as its most impressive entry.

And I loved the way humor was such a large part of the magazine. Humor doesn't get a lot of love in the magazine world. At least not the intentional kind. I still can't stop laughing at Levi Johnston's photo spread in *Playgirl*, but I don't think that was supposed to be funny.

And anytime I read a recipe in *Bon Appetit* that contains more than thirty-five ingredients, I downright guffaw. And then there are the unintentionally hilarious headlines in all those women's magazines that are forever trying to balance naughty and nice and failing on both counts. That's how you end up with headlines like "Ten Erotic Uses For Your Crock Pot (Think Long and Slow!)"

Reader's Digest can't get enough of the kidding around with its faithful little ditties found in "Humor in Uniform," "Life in These United States," and so many other blurbs and funnies sprinkled throughout like fake cheese on popcorn.

I read recently that it's virtually impossible these days to get a humor piece accepted by the *New Yorker* because the head of the editorial department, Snobby McPruneface, doesn't value humor as a genre. I got news for the *New Yorker*: I don't even *get* half those black-and-white cartoons you're so damn proud of.

Reader's Digest, on the other hand, was always the voice of the common man, the first place one could go for a quick quip that would be suitable for retelling at Rotary Club without even making the waitress blush. The headquarters is in Pleasantville, for God's sake. How can you get any more American than that?

Reader's Digest thinks it may be able to revamp its loser image by going digital, but I'm not sure that'll work since most people don't want to take their laptops into the bathroom. You can't really read *RD* anywhere else. It just wouldn't be right.

For now, bless God, the little magazine is safe thanks to declaring bankruptcy (laughing again) but if all the legal team's grand plans fail, this coffee-ringed staple of so many homes will disappear like Jell-O 1-2-3 mix and we'll have to find somewhere else to read those somewhat hysterical articles like "Eight Medical Myths!" and "Hero Pet of the Year!"

Call me thickheaded, but even with all the signs the economy was failing—double-digit unemployment, frozen credit, housing foreclosures in the thousands, a stock market in free-fall, I never really understood the depths of the recession until I read about *Reader's Digest* and, perhaps more importantly, when *Days of Our Lives* fired founding couple, John Black and Dr. Marlena Evans.

Paul Krugman's thoughtful op-ed pieces on the economy never even fazed me. Ditto my nightly hit of *Marketplace*, a thoughty economy-based show on NPR. It never hit home until Salem's wise and loving and occasionally-during-sweeps-months demon-possessed psychiatrist and her studly husband got the ax.

As everyone knows (except, possibly, readers of the *New Yorker*), John and Marlena were the unrivaled first couple of soap opera land for decades.

In a horrible injustice, the actors who portray Marlena and John were let go because they were at the top of the pay scale.

Ever since their absence, we fans have been subjected to an exceedingly icksome parade of truly bad young actors who probably just work for weed.

Why do I care so much about two TV stars that I don't even know? After all, assuming they haven't gone all crazy

Fantasia and squandered their money on white sofas and no-account cousins, John and Marlena should live out their lives in financial security that the rest of us can only dream about.

So it's not that I'm worried that they'll have to resort to putting on pizza-slice costumes and dance about by the side of the road to lure business. They won't be like my poor laid-off friend, Lanny Ray, who swears he's so poor he can't even afford to go to the Rug Doctor.

But to me, the loss of John and Marlena (as well as the potential loss of *Reader's Digest*) are two of our most important economic indicators. When networks treat soap opera royalty like Marlena and John this way, there can be no hope whatsoever for the rest of us. We are all mere weeks away from wearing our barrel-and-suspenders recessionista look on public transportation.

So, yes, I get it now. Thanks to these two longtime staples of my admittedly incredibly mediocre life.

John and Marlena have demonstrated what months of NPR, CNBC, and egghead op-ed articles by Pulitzer Prize-winning economists could not. We. Are. Doomed. As Lanny Ray would say, "The whole sitchy-ation waste-es my time and disgust-es me."

I should've seen this coming. Didn't I see all the obvious product placement tricks on *DOOL* over the past year? I specifically remember Sami Brady commenting rather clumsily to her current lover about the awesome dirt-busting ability of her new Swiffer and I immediately drove to the store and bought the regular *and* the Swiffer WetJet. Sami said they worked. And if you can't trust a former death row inmate who posed as a man in Desert Storm and later gave birth to twins with two different fathers like a damn Labrador retriever, who can you trust?

I thought that by now Marlena and John would be back, that the sponsors would realize that they must do what they could to retain Marlena (the divine Deirdre Hall) even if it meant that she would have to occasionally stare into the camera and say things like, "You know, ladies, when I need a smart pantsuit that won't break the bank, I like to shop at Kohl's. You'll find it at the intersection of value and style." She could wink, even. And then go right back into the waiting arms of John Black.

Oh, cruel economy. How can there ever be *DOOL* without them? Even as their too-long bedroom scenes began to feel about as sexy as watching your parents make out, we still adored them through all their myriad kidnappings, lost-at-seas, brainwashings, buried alives, exorcisms, and divorces. Sometimes all within the space of a few minutes.

The sour U.S. economy has managed to do what *Days* bad guy Stefano DiMeara has tried to do for more than thirty years: eliminate the Wonder Couple.

In a world that can so casually toss aside *Reader's Digest* and John and Marlena, apparently nothing is sacred.

May God have mercy on us all.

19

Menopause Spurs Thoughts of
Death and Turkey

Right now, since you ask, I'm what is known as peri-
menopausal. "Peri," some of you may know, is a Latin
prefix meaning "SHUT YOUR FLIPPIN' PIE HOLE."

There's a huge difference between perimenopause and
menopause; chiefly, during perimenopause you only think
about killing your husband three to four times a day. Kidding! I meant three to four times an *hour*.

Of course, many women in my situation try to learn as
much as they can about this stage of life. Some even embrace
and try to celebrate this phase, which can include insomnia,
memory loss, night sweats, fatigue, and memory loss (ha!). I
like to call these women *crazy people*.

Others, like me, occasionally try to find comfort by
discussing these very personal issues with trusted women

friends. Who, if you must know, leave a lot to be desired lately.

The biggest problem is that we women are competitive creatures. If you want to talk about your menopausal symptoms, your women-friends will just try to out-symptom you.

Me: "I feel like I'm losing my mind! I have these little electric currentlike hot flashes all over my body and it happens about a dozen times a day!"

BFF: "Oh, yeah? At least that's better than forgetting everything like I do. The other day, I left my kid at the dry cleaners and took my husband's shirts to see *Up*.

Me: CAN'T I JUST COMPLAIN ONE TIME WITHOUT YOU TRYING TO ONE-UP ME?"

BFF: "Shut up!"

Me: "YOU shut up! (Cue wild mood swing out of no damn where.) I'm sorry. You're the best friend I've ever had. PLEASE DON'T LEAVE ME!"

BFF: "OK, so that's not needy at all."

I can't believe I was ever friends with Angie Romano. OK, sure I can. She's the one who taught me how to look years younger in pictures. You know how when a bunch of women friends get together and get just a little sloppy drunk? A few of you even flirt inappropriately with the kinda cute Marine who has just asked you if you're a veterinarian and when you say, "No, why?" he flexes his biceps and says, "Cuz my pythons are *sick!*"

In the heat of the moment, feeling younger and friskier,

one of the posse whips out a camera and tells the waiter to, "Take our picture!" Well, Angie taught all of us how to put our arms around each other, right at the neck, and smile. So what? So this! See, each one of us reaches just under the hair-line on the back of the neck and pulls like hell on the neck skin so we *all look twenty-eight years old again*!

Try it next time you're having that ditzy, drunken photo taken. The one you'll have to beg your teenager to e-mail your old high school classmates so they can marvel at how good your neck looks. You have to ask your teen to email it because you have no idea how to do it *because you are old*.

So, really, it's hard to hate anyone who is wise enough to figure out how to make my horrendous pelican neck fat disappear for picture time.

Everyone my age likes to yak about menopause whenever we get together but I have a hard time talking or even thinking about my "females" because, let's face it: That shit is gross. When my doctor told me one time that I had a uterine polyp, I threw up on his shoes.

Maybe because he's a lot like a nerdy nine-year-old boy, TV's famous Dr. Oz thrives on the gross woman stuff. Remember the time he made Oprah hold up a big lacy-looking piece of intestinal fat for all of us to admire?

"It's called the O-mentum," he said. And while I thought that was so like the wizard that's Oz to try to kiss Oprah's ass by naming an organ after her right there on the spot, turns out that's the real name for it.

I looked up "omentum," saw a close-up picture of one, and threw up on my own shoes.

A while back, I had a little trouble with the ol' babymaker that led to a pretty significant case of anemia. And, no, you don't lose weight when you're severely anemic, which just pissed me off even more. Doesn't blood weigh anything? It seemed that at least I'd drop a few pounds from not having any.

Duh-hubby responded to my illness appropriately. For about two days. And then, on Day Three, I heard him trudge, very slowly upstairs to our bedroom, where I was lying, surrounded by empty bottles of Lipton Diet Green Tea and Nilla Wafers boxes.

"I'm . . . sooooo . . . tired . . . ," he managed before flopping onto my bedspace.

Although I looked and felt as if the entire Cullen family had been over for dinner and I was the main course, I was expected to show sympathy for *him?*

"What the hell is wrong with you?" I asked with way more concern than I actually felt.

"I gave blood today and almost passed out," he grumbled.

Now I am not proud of how poorly I reacted to this information. While it's unspeakably noble to donate blood, I selfishly wanted at least one of us to be running around with normal amounts of the stuff in our veins.

"Sooooo. . . . tired," he said again, pulling off his socks

and pants, tossing his tie and shirt onto the floor, and crawling under the covers. My covers. My anemia-wracked covers.

"Can you hand me the remote?"

Christ.

A few hours later, the NBA playoffs had worked their curative magic and Duh was feeling normal.

Me? I was still feeling as crappy as ever. If you've ever had anemia, you know exactly what I mean. Of course, because I come from a long line of hypochondriacs, I'd decided that I was dying. I'd written my last smart-ass words. This was it for me.

I told Duh that it was time to discuss my funeral, which I want to be huge and splashy, just like that one in that wonderful old movie classic, *Imitation of Life*, because that was the best funeral ever. Remember how there was a lavish funeral at the biggest church in New York featuring a gospel solo by Mahalia Jackson (who is, unfortunately, too dead to sing at my funeral but we could substitute Queen Latifah because after I saw her in *Hairspray* I knew she was up to the task). OK, so also in *Imitation of Life*, after the big, splashy funeral (at which you *will* wear a hat, assholes, this is my funeral we're talking about, show a little respect) there is a *parade* in the streets with drummers drumming and pipers piping and the body rides along in a horse-drawn hearse and it proceeds through the entire city!

And everyone cries! Just buckets and barrels of tears and the best part is when the dead woman's daughter flings herself onto the casket. I just love it when people do that at real funerals. It's so raw and real, and if at least one person doesn't fling herself or himself onto my casket and scream, "Noooo! Nooooo! Take me instead! Here! Here's my omentum! I don't need it anymore in this dark world without you!" I'm going to be completely pissed as I look down on all y'all losers. That's right. I said "down."

Maybe you don't think about your funeral, but that's how you end up with really crappy funerals where the whole thing lasts ten minutes and then somebody goes out for a bucket of Bojangles' chicken.

You will never get the anemia-induced *Imitation of Life* funeral unless you plan it. I plan to call the (snicker) "pre-planning" experts at my local funeral home and tell them I want the *Imitation of Life* special and, if they don't know what I'm talking about, they don't get my bidness.

I come from a long line of worriers, so it's not that bizarre that all this talk of anemia and menopause and omentums and such would lead to funeral planning.

The women in my family have always been chronic worriers. True story: My maternal grandmother once called the Atlanta airport to ask the pilot not to fly in a light rain because I was going to be a passenger on his plane that day. Oh yes she did.

She pleaded with the airline to spare the lives of her daughter and granddaughters, although, as memory serves, she didn't mention anything about my daddy, which was probably because he was a Democrat.

We worry about things in our control (did I unplug the coffeemaker before work?) and completely out of our control (will we get brain cancer?).

A few years ago, I realized that my favorite childhood book had been *The Three Sillies*, which is a fabulous book about how outlandish fears and worries can get in the way of living a happy, authentic life. In the book, the three sillies are a husband, wife, and daughter, who weep when they imagine that one day the daughter will have a son, and he will go into the basement to fetch some ale, and an ax might fall from a beam and kill him. None of these things has happened, mind you; it's the thought of all the awful things that could happen that makes them weep so long and hard.

I bought copies of *The Three Sillies* for Christmas presents for my sister and mother. I would've bought one for my grandmother but she had already passed by then, in her sleep, which was not how she envisioned her death, at the hands of an ax-wielding psychopath who would break into her house just after Johnny Carson went off the air.

We read selected portions of *The Three Sillies* in the same attentive, reverent manner that other families might read the Bible or Koran. After reminiscing for a few minutes, we realized all this talk of worry and death had worked up a real appetite. It was time to carve the turkey, which is Duh's responsibility every year, after he's bagged an extra five-hour midmorning nap.

As he sliced into the turkey breast, we leaned forward and our faces fell.

"It's pink," I whined.

"So?" asked Duh. "What's the big deal? We can just put it back in the oven for a few minutes if you're worried."

"Great idea. That way the bacteria can really enjoy a growth spurt in that moist heat for a few more minutes. We'll all be dead within the hour!"

The turkey was obviously riddled with botulism. What was Duh's damn problem anyway?

So we did the only responsible thing: Tossed out the turkey and ate the side dishes. Better safe than hospitalized, where, we were fairly certain, we'd never get out without contracting a horrible staph infection. Possibly in our omentums.

Maybe that all sounds silly to you, but we didn't want to take any chances. Go ahead and eat questionable turkey.

It's your funeral.

But it won't be nearly as awesome as mine. Bitches.

20

"Arf! Arf! I Just Ate My Own Shit!"

You have to wonder how Mattel came up with the idea for Puppy Tweets. Dogs using Twitter? That's the kind of idea that college students get when they're exceedingly high and everything seems to be the most brilliant idea ever conceived and they're all going to be the next Bill Gates or Jack Black.

Of course, in the cold light of day, the notion of recycling your dirty bong water to run your car doesn't seem quite as clever as it did a mere eight hours earlier, but then you also thought your pizza was plotting to kill you along about that same time.

Puppy Tweets sounds like one of those dumb-ass late-night ideas, this quirky invention that allows your dog to communicate with you about his day, his activities, his dreams.

But this time, the dumb-ass idea paid off. Puppy Tweets was a big hit when it was unveiled by Mattel recently. Who can resist a computerized toy that allows your dog to post updates to its very own Twitter page?

And, yes, I'm serious.

How does it work? Magic. No, seriously. Puppy Tweet contains a USB receiver that dog owners then connect to their computer. This allows them to download the necessary Puppy Tweets software and create a Twitter account for their dog.

When the dog moves or barks, a signal is sent from its Puppy Tweets tag to the receiver, which updates the dog's Twitter page. Owners can then check Twitter to see their dog's latest posts.

What does all this mean? That's easy. It means that, one day, it's quite possible that you'll be sitting in a very important business meeting with the high muckety-mucks at your company and you will be alerted that your dog has *just licked my balls because I can.*

Truthfully, I doubt that's one of the preprogrammed five hundred doggie tweets, but it could be.

How often can your dog tweet? Pretty damn often because Puppy Tweets works by tweeting when the sound and motion sensor on the dog collar senses barking or movement.

Which, judging by the dogs in my neighborhood, should pretty much be every minute of every day. I can't manage to tweet more than once a month and the dog across the street who's so dumb he eats his own poo, will be embracing new media like a brand-new chew toy. What is *wrong* with this picture?

Typical tweets, according to an article in the *Los Angeles Times*, include *I bark because I miss you. There. I said it. Now hurry home.* Another? *I finally caught that tail I've been chasing and . . . Ouch!*

That's certainly "awwww"-inducing, but a bit boring, am I right? Wouldn't it be much more interesting to receive a tweet from your dog that said, *Hey Doofus! You left the gate open again. So what? So this. Let's just say that Lady across the street is one might-eeeee satisfied Pomeranian.*

Or how about, *Yarf! Yarf! I just ate your kid's baseball socks and have no idea why! Let's go to the all-night vet and spend more than you make in a month! I call front seat!*

The funniest response to the announcement of Puppy Tweets has been that of honest disappointment from some dog owners that the tweets aren't "real."

As one whined to the *Times*, it's entirely possible that even though Bowser tweets that he's enjoying chasing a ball in the park, he's really just napping on top of your favorite navy blazer at home.

Uh, yeah. Because, and I hate to break this to some of you, dogs can't really talk. Except for Fly in the movie *Babe*, of course. She could totally talk, no question. But the others? Not so much.

Once again, I have to wonder why cats get short shrift. I mean if you're going to just make up stuff, why not make a Kitty Tweets for cat collars?

I'm guessing their tweets will be a bit darker. Something on the order of: *To find out who you are, you ask first what are you not. Then you are left with what you are. Oh, and the loud, slobbery thing just ate another sock. I hate my life."*

Cats never get the love that dogs do, and this vexes me. Especially in light of a new study that discovered that cats do a lot more than you think when they're left home alone.

I know what you're thinking. Cello playing, right? Nooooo, but close.

Thanks to a study by cat scientists (not actual cats as scientists; that would be nuts, besides the fact that they don't make lab coats that small), we now know that house cats do a lot more than sleep while their humans are away.

And they're not passively fake tweeting. Using strategically positioned "cat cams," programmed to take photos every fifteen minutes and attached to the collars of fifty (I'm guessing seriously pissed off) house cats, the cat scientists were able to determine that cats actually only spend about 6 percent of their time sleeping. I have three cats and they've basically been asleep since Boy George was popular so this is shocking, to put it mildly.

Cat cameras revealed that cats spent 22 percent of their days looking out the window, 12 percent playing with other pets, and 8 percent climbing on furniture. The rest of the time, they did things like watch TV (because they believe their leader, Tyra Banks, is speaking to them personally). TV viewing accounted for 6 percent of a typical house cat's day, the exact same amount as "hiding under a table," presumably when *The Marriage Ref* was on.

Sometimes, the cats watched DVDs, which is a puzzler. I mean, I get how they can work the remote, but even those of us with opposable thumbs usually pry the case open with so much force that the DVD pops out, sails across the room and under the couch, never to be seen again. I've still got the neighbor's *Slumdog Millionaire* collecting dust bunnies under my couch somewhere, along with some old Disney princess movies and, quite possibly, The Wiggles.

During the very same news cycle, it should be noted, there was a heartwarming story about a dog who alerted his wheelchair-bound owner to the fire raging through their duplex by barking and pulling him to safety.

Firefighters said the dog deserved a commendation for saving the man's life. Look, I hate to break bad yet again on dogs but why doesn't anyone ever consider that maybe the fire *started* because of the attention-mongering dog. Maybe it was the *dog* who left that cigarette to smolder in the recliner cushions. Hmm?

Meanwhile, across the way, I'm imagining a cat spending part of its 22 percent of the day staring at the leaping flames and making a sarcastic sad-face at the dog while holding a phone that he has just punched only a nine and a one into.

"Want me to call for help, asshole?" the cat asks. "Oops, too late. Time for my cello lesson. But, no worries. You can tweet someone about it and maybe they can help. Yeah, that'll work. Did I mention I hate my life?"

Puppy Tweets will probably lead to all sorts of social networking for the dog world. Maybe dogs (and cats) will be on Facebook before too long, "poking" one another, playing silly Mafia Wars, and taking lame-ass quizzes to find out which member of the Village People they are. They'll send one another imaginary food and drinks, and even sneak around trying to hook up with old lovers. (And they'll always put pictures of themselves as pups when you know they're at least 120 in you-know-what years.)

They'll even post their "Random Twenty-five Facts" about themselves but, because they're dogs, will probably lose interest after about twelve and go sniff another dog's ass.

I realize that it's trendy to put down Facebook (or, as Aunt Sudavee insists on calling it "The Facebook"). And I am nothing if not trendy.

I have a sort of fragile relationship with Facebook. The truth is, my cats would do a better job of keeping up with all their Facebook friends.

Status updates should come naturally to someone who makes her living with, uh, whatchamacallit, words. But, like my documented tweeting problems, updating Facebook is also challenging. I don't want to be like the dullard who writes simply, *I like grape jelly!* Which would only be interesting if she added, *in my shoes.* So I worry and fret and end up posting nothing at all rather than risk posting a mediocre status update.

I admire Facebooks friends who are committed to putting it all out there. Face it, some status updates can be wrenchingly poignant. I'm thinking in particular of these: *"My husband of 25 years is in a coma* and *I hear NBC may cancel* Friday Night Lights *again.*

And even a Facebooking dog wouldn't have done the dumb thing I did one time, causing my precious niece, Lucy, to defriend me. Apparently it's a violation of trust to say things like, "Dude! How drunk *were* you at that sorority party?" with her parents right there at the dinner table.

Awkward silence ensued and Lucy wisely restricted my profile to the utterly useless limits of viewing a few carefully edited photos of her involved in wholesome study sessions and reading about the Facebook environmental groups she had just joined.

Having violated the sanctity of the aunt/niece trust, I now was subjected to reading about a young woman whose college experience was about as exciting as mildew.

A cat would've never let such a thing happen. Cats are mysterious creatures who never betray another's trust. So now I'm officially an asshat in my lovely niece's eyes. Which looked just a little bloodshot the last time I saw her, just saying.

With Puppy Tweets' success, I predict more pet owners

will set up blogs for their beloved animals who, I fervently hope, will figure out how to illustrate their blogs with charming photos of humans drinking out of toilets for a change. Don't you imagine that your pets are sick and tired of all those pictures on your blogs showing them in "hilarious" positions?

A blog, to those of you who are named either Ezra or Zeke, is short for "weblog" which is Latin for "nothing good on TV." There is even a "blogosphere," which has replaced Pluto in the solar system and is peopled by many millions of life-forms that want to share endlessly about their lives and emotions. Some of them are scary-good, others read like a dog could've written them.

My favorite name for a dog's blog would be on the lines of "My Name is Fido and I CRAP Excellence." Yeah, that's pretty perfect.

21

Meat'normous?
Now That's Just Wrong

This Christmas, while watching that saptastic old movie, *It's A Wonderful Life* with Duh for the twentieth consecutive year, I was reminded of all the people I'm glad were born. As you know, *Life* is all about showing how one person's life, no matter how seemingly ordinary, can have extraordinary purpose and impact. I found myself particularly grateful for Dr. Jonas Salk for keeping us healthy and for Eric Clapton for giving us *Layla* and to Papa Murphy for inventing a decent take-and-bake pizza.

The movie, which usually puts me to sleep long before Zuzu gets her wings or whatever, could use some updating to make it more relevant. Blasphemy, you say? Mayhaps. But think of the fun we could have in the casting.

Obviously, our old pal Bernie Madoff would be a perfect

sub for the movie's miserly cheat, Mr. Potter. He lived to screw the worker bees out of their hard-earned money despite the valiant efforts of sad-sack do-gooder George Bailey, portrayed so memorably by Jimmy Stewart.

I wouldn't want to recast George because, honestly, when Jimmy Stewart finally snaps and gets his drink on, beats up the newel, yells (rightfully, if you ask me) at his annoying-ass kids, and chews out an innocent schoolteacher on that wacky tin can-and-string telephone, no one could do it better. To put it another way, for someone who's supposed to be so damn nice and decent, George Bailey goes from zero to complete douche in record time.

Chinless wonder Joe Lieberman could reprise the role of Mr. Gower, the distracted druggist who couldn't concentrate on uninsured people who need medicine and instead, sent home a nice bag of poison for them to take.

Life is unwittingly hilarious in places. Every year, I wake up long enough to laugh out loud at the agonized look on George Bailey's face when he's told that, because he'd never been born, his beloved Mary was "an old maid, George."

This is revealed in the same horror-soaked tones as if she had succumbed to leprosy or become a Civil War reenactor. To underscore that, the lovely Donna Reed is given Coke-bottle glasses to wear and stripped of all makeup. Because that's how all unmarried women looked back before Photoshop, I guess.

The other funny thing—though, again, unintentional—is

the movie's nutty insistence that Pottersville was somehow inferior to Bedford Falls, a place so relentlessly pristine and virtuous that it would make Garrison Keillor's Lake Wobegon look like Amesterdam's fabled weed-and-whores district. Music, dancing, drinking, gambling? The residents of Pottersville appeared to be having, in redneck parlance, "a large time." Toss in a little Cirque du Soleil and some white tigers and it was practically Vegas.

George Bailey was kind but repressed and lacked balance in life. When his job tanked, thanks to the actions of his weepy, loony-tunes uncle (obviously we are casting Glenn Beck), he went apeshit. If we learn nothing else from the movie, we should learn (1) that you can guilt trip a whole town into rescuing you from financial ruin if you haven't been too big of a sonovabitch and (2) sometimes you really do need to tell the kid banging on the piano to shut the hell up.

My annual viewing of *It's A Wonderful Life* reminds me why Christmas is, like the song says, the most wonderful time for a beer. Three days before Christmas, I was once again doing the whole buying-and-wrapping-at-the-last-minute thing.

My friend, Claire, informed me that she'd finished shopping back in August.

"I did everything online," she chirped. Of course, I was too kind to point out that except for the homebound elderly who have no choice, no one should ever give every single person on their gift list a fleece hoodie from Lands' End. Where's the creativity in that? Still, I have to admit that it was smart to surf and click and smugly await deliveries at normal, non-Sopranos-like freight costs. Smart, but boring!

I wanted Claire to wait in line with me at Walmart, where there was a line of a couple dozen people smelling of cigarette smoke, fried fish, and desperation. Which, now that I think about it, is pretty much what it would smell like if you could *bottle* my twenties. Starter marriage, small town, long story, you get the idea.

And it never fails that when you finally get to the cashier, you're behind yet another grown adult who is slowly and laboriously writing out a check that is decorated with Disney characters. They must then fish out a couple of forms of ID while, once again, I scratch my noggin and wonder why they don't just use a debit card.

To these fellow travelers on life's journey, may I just say that I totally get that someone told you that someone told them that someone else told their cousin who once worked as a security guard at a bank that debit cards aren't safe and that there are hordes of crooks out there waiting to get ahold of your PIN and steal your identity. But trust me, nobody really wants to be you. If you think about it, it's pretty egotistical of you to think so.

Face it. You're a woman in your fifties and you have Disney princesses parading across your antique legal tender. If somebody's going to get her ID stolen, it's probably somebody way cooler than you.

Back in August, when I should've begun my shopping, the

merchandise selection was probably better. Those purple leopard-print UGGs the Princess was pining for somehow morphed into black vinyl closed-toe bedroom shoes with a nifty red-plaid lining. And, yes, she was pissed. It didn't even help that I'd scrawled "Team Edward" on one toe and "Team Jacob" on the other. Nothing could quite eliminate that nursing home vibe. I was so busted.

For Duh there was, of course, only one choice by the time I got around to doing my Christmas shopping: Burger King's new Flame meat-scented cologne was a steal at just $3.99 plus tax. The silver spray bottle embossed with a red heart is perfect for any man who wants to wear, as Burger King brags, "the scent of seduction with a hint of flame-broiled meat." I swear I am not making this up.

You might wonder why Burger King is getting into the fragrance business, but I say why not? It's not like the whole fast-food thing has worked out that well for them.

Besides, Celine Dion and David Beckham sell their cheap smell'um at Walmart, so why not the ubiquitous and somewhat pervy Burger King? And Flame is a whole lot easier to say than something classy that has inserts in fancy magazines like Acqua Di Gio Pour Homme, which, if my high school French is correct, and I'm fairly certain it is, means "Water of God for My Homies." Yeah, I'm bilingus.

Burger King saved my 98-percent-fat bacon by rolling out Flame in time for the holidays.

The commercial featured the comically big-headed,

spray-tanned King peddling his cologne while wearing only a crown and a faux fur loincloth as Barry White-ish music plays in the background. Nah, none of that is weird.

And while some have said this cologne gig was just a clever Christmas marketing gimmick for BK, others actually like the smell of Flame. None other than The Honorable Kathie Lee Gifford herself squealed her approval after spritzing a reluctant cameraman with Flame on her *After the Real Today Show, The Part That No One Watches*. It's only a matter of time before Frank Gifford introduces his new signature scent for the holidays: Old Man's Stinky Football Jersey.

A lot of people find the King completely creepy but Burger King is loyal to its mascot and even exploits his royal weirdness. When he's not dousing himself in Flame and offering to "set the mood no matter what mood you're in the mood for" (say whaaaat?), the King is at the center of a breakfast menu ad campaign that includes, or did I just dream this, a commercial in which he crawls into bed with a startled young man and cheerfully offers him a "Meat'normous" sandwich.

Pass.

We shouldn't be surprised by the odd ad campaign, given an earlier one for Whopper Virgins, in which real-life Thai villagers, rural Romanian farmers, and tundra-dwellers from Greenland are asked to compare the Whopper to a Big Mac from McDonald's.

The commercials make me feel mildly uncomfortable, rather like the painful moments on *Survivor* when the air-headed contestants try to look honestly interested during the obligatory segment when they must interact with island natives and visit holy shrines and stuff.

In the BK commercials, the bemused villagers prefer the Whopper (duh) but I think that's probably only because somebody threw in a few cases of Flame.

So, Christmas was kind of a bust in the present department this year. Duh wasn't nearly as taken with the ironic nature of his gift as I thought he would be. And the Princess is still pouting over her nursing home-slash-vampire shoes.

As we gathered around the TV to watch *Life* yet again on Christmas night, I reminded both of them that Christmas isn't about presents. It's about being together as a family to celebrate Jesus' birth and to remember the true spirit of the season. Of course, this didn't go over as well as you might imagine, since I was, at that selfsame moment, absentmindedly twirling my present, *a just over one full carat diamond eternity ring* (Score! At last!) on my left ring finger. When I opened it on Christmas morning, the first thing I said to Duh, because we'd just seen the movie *Blood Diamond* and had discussed its globally and socially responsible message, was "Is this a blood diamond? Because I want to make absolutely sure that this is 100 percent cruelty-free before I put it on my hand." Duh looked real confused. Apparently he'd forgotten all about the movie in the week and a half since we'd seen it.

"I-I-I-'m not really sure. . . . I guess so. . . . I hope so. . . ." He looked downright scared.

I let him twist in the wind for another second or so before I busted out laughing.

"Oh, honey, I'm just messin' wid ya. I don't care if you had to cut off Leo DiCaprio's *head* to get this thing, it's *FREAKIN' GORGEOUS!!!*"

Duh beamed and the smell of flame-broiled meat filled the living room. I'm pretty sure we can all agree on one thing: It's a wonderful thing that Duh was born.

Now, because I do want to give something to all y'all, I'm going to share my Can't Miss Christmas Morning Breakfast Strata recipe. Y'all know me: It's super good and super easy.

CHRISTMAS MORNING BREAKFAST STRATA-GY

6 cups cubed French bread (1 loaf, usually)

1 pound sausage (I like Jimmy Dean sage but you can use any flavor you prefer), cooked and drained

2 cups shredded sharp cheddar (just buy it pre-shredded; it's Christmas. Don't you have a bike to assemble or something?)

2 green onions, chopped (yes, tops, too)

1 quart half-and-half

9 large eggs

1 teaspoon dry mustard

1 teaspoon salt

Pepper, hot sauce and/or Worcestershire sauce to taste

Grease a good-size rectangular casserole dish with butter. Spread bread cubes evenly in the dish. Top with (in order) sausage, cheese, and chopped onions, sprinkling each evenly over bread cubes.

Lightly mix together half-and-half, eggs, mustard, salt, and spices. Pour liquid mixture over bread/sausage/cheese, cover with foil and let sit in fridge overnight. Preheat oven to 350 degrees and bake, lightly covered with foil, for about 45 minutes. Cut into squares and serve with fruit (I like those big bowls of presliced fruit from Costco) and store-bought miniature cinnamon muffins. Low effort, big raves, trust me.

Serves 8-10

22

I Dreamed A Dream That My Lashes Were Long

I get a little cheesed every time I think about Susan Boyle, the Scottish singing sensation. I'm not mad at her, of course. What bugs me is how everybody was so surprised that a matronly chick in a dowdy lace dress could sing pretty.

Not since Gomer Pyle's singing genius was discovered while changing a tire in Mayberry have so many been so shocked that a homely person could make beautiful music.

But, really, why?

Why were so many people so surprised that a plump middle-aged woman of daffy disposition could have real talent? Beauty and talent don't always, or even often, go together. (See Simpson, comma, Jessica; bless her heart.)

With her bushy brows arching toward heaven, Susan

Boyle sang her lumpy ass off and a British talent-show judge proclaimed that it was the surprise of his life.

Why is that?

Say what you will about Mick Jagger, whom I adore, but he ain't purty. He's a wormy looking little fella with tragic features but, sha-zam, is he talented! And, to most, a sexy senior. Cause he's a boy.

The way the Brits carried on so about Susan Boyle's bold decision to commit the offense of SWU (Singing While Unattractive) was tiresome, but it would've been even worse if she'd made her debut on *American Idol*, I suppose.

Randy: "Dang, that was good! Holler at cha! Little pitchy and you're no looker and it was the wrong song choice, but it was good! Dawg."

Paula: "Oh my goodness, you just came out there and really, well, the angels and the ozone and everything just really brought together a thing that is, well, just such a thing that is just so beautiful in a sort of symbiotic eternity. And you can't help how you look."

Kara: "Can anybody please just pronounce my name right? Please? My name? Anybody? Oh, and you on stage? Yeah, I really think that you should know that I prefer my contestants to be hot eighteen-year-old guys so, uh, yeah, well, this was kind of a time-waster for me."

Simon: "Look, the elephant in the room is, well, it's bloody *her*. The bottom line is this woman is painfully, undeniably, and unalterably unattractive, and we live in a shallow culture that simply can't support a woman who chooses to wear such a ghastly Kmart frock to perform in a nationally televised performance where I'm forced to look at her."

It's regrettable that women have to worry so much about appearance. Even Ellen DeGeneres, who replaced poor Paula, freeing her to pursue other projects, is obsessed with her looks, otherwise why would she agree to be the newest spokesmodel for CoverGirl cosmetics? (BTW, "pursuing other projects" is Hollywood-speak for rehab followed by another painful reality show.)

It's a little curious. Ellen never seemed to care about conventional stuff like foundation and powder. She was the comedic version of Susan Boyle, talented without fretting about the whole looks thing.

But turns out she was a little worried about it and now, suddenly, she's everywhere, on magazines, the sides of buses, on TV, yakking about CoverGirl's new Simply Ageless Foundation.

I usually pay big bucks for department store foundation so this was pretty tempting, the notion that I could use something to give me a flawless face that was available at CVS and cost less than a medium pizza. Ellen told me it was so, and she wouldn't lie, would she? Besides, who among us doesn't want to look like a fifty-year-old lesbian?

If this cheap drugstore foundation was responsible for

Ellen's glowing skin, then that was good enough for me. Not to mention Susan Boyle, but only if she wants to gussy up a bit. She could still sing the paint off the walls.

I don't have a great set of pipes going for me so I cling to the little things. Which is why I couldn't wait to get Simply Ageless home. It was so cute in its little purple compact with a swirl of white antiaging goo mixed right in.

Unfortunately, I couldn't get the damn thing open. After about fifteen minutes, I finally pried the bottom section open and a cute little white applicator sponge rolled out. OK . . . but how to get the foundation part open?

The CoverGirl Web site was there to help. At first, I felt pretty stupid being unable to open a simple compact but then I saw "How to Open Simply Ageless" as a clickable link at the Web site so I figured there were hundreds, if not thousands, of middle-aged women out there frustrated as hell in their pursuit to look like Ellen DeGeneres.

There were three steps, mostly involving twisting counter-clockwise, clockwise, rotating bottoms and tops, and quoting Chaucer while balancing plates on a stick and scratching your ass.

I was kidding about the Chaucer part. 'Nother words: I just couldn't get the damn thing open. I imagine Susan Boyle would've given the whole project about six seconds before hollering "Bollocks!" and gone out to shear the sheep or rethatch the roof or whatever people do in Scotland when they're not singing on the telly or carping about the weather.

After a few more minutes of wrestling with the compact, I broke down and called the toll-free CoverGirl help line, where a perky sounding beauty consultant said she'd be happy to help once I described my dilemma.

"You have to turn it counter-clockwise on the clear part while grasping the bottom purple part."

"Do I have to do the Chaucer part now?"

"Excuse me?"

"Kidding. Please continue. I tried all that stuff and nothing happened."

There was a brief pause and the phone had that dead-air sound that made me think she'd put me on hold so she could laugh out loud at the hick in North Carolina who couldn't open the stupid compact.

Finally, she came back on the line, perky as ever.

"Ma'am, maybe you could ask someone who is stronger than you in the household to open it for you?"

WTF?????

"I'm not some weakling," I sputtered. "Just because I don't have Ellen's guns and I really need that Olay regenerative serum doesn't mean anything."

"Of course you're not weak," the consultant said, clearly thinking that I was, too.

"Take it back."

"Excuse me?"

"Look, I really want to use this product today. I've got a meeting and I need to look sixteen years younger by two o'-clock."

"OK," she said, brightly. I could just picture her making big circles in the air beside her temple while she talked to me. "Perhaps you could gently rap the compact on a countertop. Some people find that helpful."

"What if I *just take a freakin' hammer to it?*"

Suddenly, she sounded serious, not at all perky and more than a little frightened.

"Ma'am, we at CoverGirl most certainly do not advise that you do that."

Empowered, I decided to be an even bigger bitch.

"What if I put it in the driveway and roll over it repeatedly with my car?"

Silence.

"Fire all of my guns at once and explode into space?"

"Ma'am, that's from *Born to Be Wild*."

I had underestimated my foe. She clearly had a grip on late '60s Steppenwolf, so how bad could she be? Maybe I did need a stronger member of the household to help me.

Just as quickly, she told me that she'd mail me a coupon for a new compact or the CoverGirl product of my choice (their waterproof mascara is the best ever). But now, she needed to go. I'm guessing there was a large-pore emergency brewing on the West Coast.

I think Susan Boyle had it right all along. I'm sick of trying to shave the years off with all these little pots of goo that clutter my vanity. Think of the very name of that piece of furniture: vanity. Why shouldn't it be something more evolved? Like my self-assured or my self-esteem? While Susan has gotten a tiny makeover, she's still her haggis-enjoying self and I could learn a lot from that.

It's doubtful Susan Boyle has even thought about her eyelash sitchy-ation. Long lashes are a big deal these days, at least to Latisse spokesmodel Brooke Shields.

I probably won't buy Latisse because it's prescription only and that just seems like a lot of trouble. Besides, the endless warnings of possible side effects that should include unrelenting hotness and maybe X-ray vision but really include discolored eyelids and itchiness make it less tempting.

Latisse, a pretty name that'll probably show up in kindergartens across this great land in about five years, is manufactured by the same company that gave us Botox. (Another product which Authentic Woman Susan Boyle knows nothing about.)

Latisse started out as a glaucoma remedy but got renamed and repackaged ($120 for a month's worth) after its magical lash-lengthening properties were discovered by accident.

I repeat: When did we become so obsessed with our eyelashes? Maybelline has a new vibrating mascara. Is it a sex toy or a lash lengthener? You be the judge.

Pulse Perfection mascara looks cool, but I'm plenty

apprehensive about sticking a rod that vibrates at "7,000 times per stroke" that close to my eyeball. What if my hand slips during the application? Would it jackhammer my brain? I'd hate to lobotomize myself in the lame, insane pursuit of beauty. What would I do? Just sit at my self-esteem every day staring vacantly at the mirror and wondering why I sat there in the first place.

Let's stop the madness! Eyelashes are designed to keep crud out of your eyes (medical definition), or to be batted seductively at the object of one's affections (my definition), or to be pulled out one by one in an obsessive-compulsive manner (Sylvia Plath's definition).

I believe that clears everything up. Dawgs.

23

Marriage in Three Acts

Act I

The front desk clerk warned us about the minibar in our room as soon as we checked into our Vegas hotel for the week.

"I have to tell you something," he said in a tone as serious as if Wayne Newton had just up and died in the Dale Chihuly glass-flowered lobby of the Bellagio. "The minibar is hyper-sensitive and it will charge you sometimes if it detects even the slightest motion when you approach it."

Because duh-hubby and I share an irrational disdain for overpriced snack foods, we gave the desktop minibar a wide berth once we got in our gorgeous lake-view room. Yeah, we paid the extry $30 for the view because it was our twentieth anniversary, and we read in the hotel brochure that if you have a lake-view room, you can see the water fountains shoot up in time to music on your TV every twenty minutes. It is sooooo worth it.

Brushing by the minibar to play with the electronically controlled drapes because I am, at heart, a Clampett, Duh fairly screamed at me.

"You're getting too close to the mini bar! Didn't you hear what the desk clerk said? Do you want to spend nine bucks for a pack of peanut M&Ms? DO YOU????"

Hmmm. Maybe renewing our vows wasn't such a good idea after all.

Duh was so paranoid about the minibar that, watching him dart by it, I was reminded of Tom Cruise in *Mission Impossible* when he did back flips and even caught his own sweat droplets to keep from setting off the laser alarms. But seriously? Army-crawling on the carpet just to avoid setting off insanely overpriced Fiji Water? This was not the romantic scene I envisioned when I made the reservations.

Our first trip to Vegas was an eye-opener, and not just because of those wicked cool electric drapes. For starters, it's in the middle of nowhere. There's desolate mountains, hundreds of miles of cactus-studded desert and then-bam!-it's GIRLS! GIRLS! GIRLS! and ALL-U-CAN-EAT CRAB LEGS!

Cruising across town in our complimentary white stretch limo enroute to the Graceland Wedding Chapel to renew our vows before Elvis, we were momentarily delayed as a heatstroke victim was loaded into an ambulance. A walleyed tourist drinking rum punch from a life-size plastic guitar with a straw attached stopped to take pictures. Second weirdest sight: an attractive woman limping into a casino wearing a full leg cast *and* high heels.

It was early May but already the temperature hovered around a hundred by the time we got to the Graceland chapel, where a sign out front announced "WHERE JON BON JOVI AND BILLY RAY CYRUS GOT MARRIED," although, it should be noted, not to each other. I don't think. In the early-afternoon heat, we were wilting faster than our $7 airplane salads, so we scurried inside.

Fortunately, inside Graceland the air-conditioning was cranked up good. We had to wait for a minute while the young woman at the reception desk finished hot-gluing some silk flowers onto a rental veil. We were getting remarried at 2:30 P.M., to duplicate exactly our wedding twenty years ago. What can I tell y'all? I'm romantic as shit.

I was getting a little nervous that Elvis was going to be late but, at 2:20 exactly, he walked in, looking very much alive, and mumbled some Elvis-style pleasantries.

He led us into the chapel and, never once breaking character, grabbed a microphone and sang *Can't Help Falling in Love With You*. Then he threw the mic down and sprinted from his pulpit to walk me down the aisle. He then tossed me off to Duh and jumped back in the pulpit. I was blown away: Elvis was wedding singer, preacherman, and father of the bride, all in one.

Elvis read the vows, which included several wonderfully

cheesy song references. Duh vowed to *Love Me Tender* and I promised to never send him to *Heartbreak Hotel*.

After it was over, Elvis presented us with our marriage certificate *and* a replica of his and Priscilla's, which I thought was a little egotistical but it didn't cost any more so it was OK. We posed for pictures, me, Duh, and Elvis, as though the three of us had just been married. I clutched my complimentary three-rose bouquet and Duh wore a red rose boutonniere that also came with our "Viva Las Vegas" package.

Before he could leave the building, I just had to tell Elvis that I truly loved his black, sparkly jumpsuit.

"Had to smash up a Trans Am or two to make this one, darlin'," he said. I knew right away that he said that about eighty times a day, but it didn't matter. Elvis's sidekick and photographer collected the money. Elvis is too classy to take it himself and merely ducked out a side door when I tried to tip him, which I thought was just so very Elvis.

The limo took us back to the Bellagio where we got gussied up for Cirque du Soleil's *Love* show. For those of you who don't speak French, Cirque du Soleil is French for "Buford, you're 'bout to see some weird shit!"

Our twentieth anniversary evening ended exactly as it had twenty years before, with me watching SportsCenter while Duh dozed peacefully, and me waking him up to show him basketball highlights.

"Which is why we work," he has said on more than one occasion.

Amen to that, and to twenty more. . . .

Act II

We also work because Duh is nothing like Richard Batista. Who he, you ask?

Dr. Batista is the doctor you may have read about who must have skipped bioethics class the week they discussed whether or not it was cool to donate a kidney to your dying wife and then try to take it back when she dumped you.

Although I can sympathize with the whole man-spurned angle (wifey reportedly took up with her karate instructor after getting all healthy and whole again), it's tacky beyond words to ask the mother of your children to please return the kidney you gave her like it's your favorite piece of Corningware and your so-called best friend is just bound and determined to keep "forgetting" to return it even though she's had it since her aunt died last August and you really need it back to make a proper funeral tetrazzini. Oh, sorry. Where was I?

Yes, Dr. Batista. Well, I do sympathize with him because it's a wretched thought that your very own kidney, that which hath filtered countless kegs of beer through undergrad and medical school, now enables your ex to toss back Mai Tais with her new boyfriend after a few hours of breaking bricks with their foreheads or whatever.

Here's the thing, though, Doc. Sure, you've got a nasty scar to remind you of what you used to have, but trust me, getting that kidney back won't make you feel any better. I mean not for more than a week or two, anyway. Those two weeks, you'd probably be on top of the world, but seriously, no longer than that.

Lawyers got involved and the doc decided he didn't want the kidney back so much as he wanted its value, which he decided was $1.5 million. Which kinda makes those home parties where you get a few twenties for your old gold necklaces look like chump change, right?

The real problem with this is that it turns out, you can't put a price tag on a vital organ. Which is why they call it organ *donation* not organ selling. When you go to renew your driver's license and they ask you if you're an organ donor, they don't mean there's a guy out back with a couple of reasonably clean knives who can give you some serious cash if you want to get rid of an organ today. ("What's it gonna take to get you to give up that pancreas to-*day*, lil lady?")

Donating body parts is at the tippy-top of things to do to get into heaven. I don't care what else you've done wrong; you give somebody a kidney, those pearly gates will swing wide. (Which is why Tiger Woods might want to think about letting go of a lung or something before too long.)

Dr. Batista's wife is lucky she doesn't have my kidney 'cause I'd camp outside that karate studio going, "Karate? Are you kidding me? I don't think *our* kidney can take that. And lay off those sugary sodas, would you?"

Act III

In the third act of our marriage play, allow me to vent just a moment about a couple that may love each other a little too much.

Please tell me that I'm not the only person who thinks Pat and Gina Neely, the nauseatingly in love stars of Food Network's *Down Home with the Neelys*, need to get a room. With a velvet swing, mirrors, and plenty of oils that aren't Crisco.

Pat and Gina Neely host a cooking show but they baby talk, kiss, and cuddle so much that it's a wonder anything gets cooked.

And, yes, I could turn it off but then I'd miss the only soft porn I get all week—plus I'm incapable of turning off a show that promises a recipe for macaroni and cheese topped with strips of bacon and crushed potato chips. In-cape-uh-bull.

So the food is fabulously, decadently Southern, but the banter? Well, this is only a slight exaggeration:

Pat: "Today, Gina and I arc gonna make some barbecued ribs that'll set your mouth on fire!"

Gina: "*You* set my mouth on fire, baby, oooh, ooooooh."

Pat: "Oh, girl, when you talk like that, I can't remember whether I put the vanilla extract in the sweet potatoes or not."

Gina: "Baby, I'm the only sweet you need. Come over here and gimme some sugar!"

(Camera nervously lingers on a pan of mashed rutabagas languishing by the sink while sounds of "Mmmmm, oooh, baby" come from somewhere near the Mixmaster stand.)

Pat: "We're back! And it's time to stuff that duck!"

Gina: "You the only duck I wanna stuff!"

Pat: "Baby, I don't even know what that means but it sounds like it might be hot!"

Gina: "Mmmmm, Pat, come over here and watch me lick this spoon."

Pat: "Girl, I wish I *was* that spoon."

Gina *(to camera)*: "My husband is so baaaaaad, isn't he ladies? You know I like to keep my man happy and one way I do that is with my crème brulee."

Pat: "Was that French? Cause, baby, you know I like French. French toast. French fries. French kisses! Mmmm, put that turkey dressing pan down, girl, and get over here!"

Gina: "Down, boy! We have to keep our minds on what's cooking."

Pat: "I'd hit that."

Gina: "What?"

Pat: "Oh, sorry. I was just daydreaming 'bout the time I first saw you back in middle school and you were so fine and my best friend, Rodney, asked me what I thought of you. . . ."

Gina: "Pat! That's enough sessy talk for one day. This butternut squash isn't going to sauté itself, now is it?"

Pat: "I'd like you to butter my nuts. . . ."

(*Hasty commercial break*)

Gina (*visibly disheveled*): "And we're back and, whoa! Who's that at the door? Why it's Pat's noseybutt mama. Again."

NBM: "Y'all cuttin' the fool up in here *again*? (*to Pat*): "I told you this triflin' heifer was gonna be the death of you. . . ."

Gina: "Why you old . . ."

Pat (*separating the two*): "Join us next time when Mama shows Gina how to clean the oven by sticking her head in it with the gas on. Mama, you sure that's safe?"

NBM: "Oh, yes, honey. It's the *only* way."

Everybody always says that marriage is such hard work but I don't believe that. All you need to get along through any disagreement is this Marriage-Saving Blueberry Pie, courtesy of my friend Jana. One bite and all will be forgiven.

I DON'T CARE WHAT YOU DID, JUST GIMME SOME MORE OF THAT PIE, PIE

Crust:
1 and one-half cups graham cracker crumbs
2 tablespoons sugar
Pinch salt
1 stick butter

Melt the butter in a heavy saucepan and add the other ingredients. Blend with a fork and press evenly onto the bottom and sides of a greased 9-inch pie pan. Bake 8 minutes at 325 degrees. Cool completely.

Cream Cheese Filling:
8 ounces cream cheese, softened
⅓ cup sugar
1 teaspoon vanilla
2 eggs

Combine cream cheese, sugar, and vanilla and beat until smooth. Add eggs and beat well again. Pour into pie shell and bake at 325 degrees until filling is set, about 30 minutes. Remove and let cool completely.

While that's cooling, mix up this divine and simple

Blueberry Glaze
2 cups blueberries
½ cup water
⅓ cup sugar

Combine in saucepan; bring to boil; reduce heat; simmer, covered 5 minutes, stirring once. Remove from heat and add 1 ½ tablespoons cornstarch mixed with 2 tablespoons cold water.

This will thicken things up nicely. Bring back to boil and cook 1 more minute, stirring constantly. Remove from heat; let cool until tepid. Spoon blueberry glaze on top of cheese pie. Chill at least 1 hour. Enjoy!

24

Politically Correct:
A Palin/La Toya Ticket

ver since I first watched them join hands high in the air together at various stops on the campaign trail, I pictured the Obamas and the Bidens as the Ricardos and the Mertzes.

They're a congenial foursome but it's not always a blissful relationship. One gets the distinct impression that if they went to Hollywood on vacation, the Bidens would somehow end up being the ones to accidentally land a cream pie in William Holden's face at the Brown Derby and the Obamas would be apologizing for it while making it very clear that there would be no talent night at the Babalu for either Jill or Joe. Everybody say, "Waaaaaaahhhhhh."

The Bidens remind me of the Mertzes. He tends to shoot off his mouth; she tends to rush to his side and defend him.

Together, the Bidens have a vexing "Did I just say that out loud?" quality about them.

I wonder if Obama has ever second-guessed asking Joe Biden to be his veep. A jolly, tail-wagging foil for Obama's crisp demeanor, Biden occasionally seems Lucy-like. Some of the stuff he comes up with (remember how he told us he'd never let anyone he loved board an airplane during flu season?) makes it sound as if he's been hitting the Vitameatavegamin pretty hard.

When Biden commits a gaffe (which would make a pretty terrific drinking game) you'll see Obama maintain a steely gaze and discreetly pinch his elbow. It's the same gesture that Ricky used when Lucy was about to make a pure-T fool out of herself in front of Milton Berle. (Ask your parents.) And it's the same gesture that every mom uses during a church service to get her squirmy kid to be quiet and sit up straight.

Biden doesn't have any trouble sitting up straight, but being quiet is another matter. Not as hard as packaging candy on an assembly line with a broken conveyor belt, mind you, but still pretty hard.

Biden is a yappy and irrepressible sort. It wouldn't surprise me to see video of him and first dog Bo happily romping and yelping amongst Michelle's freshly planted lemongrass. Michelle, who seems elegant but somewhat boring, would rap on the kitchen window and shake her head "no" to get them to stop. Yes, there would be lots of splainin' to do later.

And while we're talking about first ladies, wouldn't it be

wonderful if we had one who we could really relate to? A gal pal for us all? I get so sick of the monotonous do-gooders that we've had in the past. Just once, I'd like to see a sweats-wearin' redneck first lady. Feet on the Lincoln coffee table while she's interviewed by *Family Circle Gardens Bazaar* or whomever.

"My outfit? Oh, yeah. It's by Hanes. Want some more boiled peanuts with your saltines?"

"My beauty regimen? Two words: Oil of Olay."

"My legacy? Well, let's see, Lady Bird had beautification, Betty Ford had rehab, Laura Bush had literacy, Rosalynn Carter had houses for poor people . . . hmmm, is free lottery tickets for kids under twelve taken?"

We tend to focus on the Obama presidency because it seemed as if the Bush years would never, ever end. And now they have and so we celebrate, sort of, with a lot more kitsch than Bush ever had. I'm remembering the Obama Inauguration Genuine Embossed Champagne Bottle that came complete with your name in script as a "witness to history." Never mind that the only witnessing you did was to look up at the overhead TV at Applebee's during 50-cent wings hour on Inauguration Day.

You could pour that "elixir of hope" into a limited-edition commemorative wine glass etched with the faces of Obama and Biden before enjoying a rousing game of table tennis using your officially sanctioned Obama inaugural Ping-Pong paddle.

All the commercialism did chafe a bit, but probably not as much as the Obama Age of Hope thong. There were even, for a short time, Obama condoms which came with the advice to "Use good judgment" on the side of the box. And don't forget the Yes, We Can! (opener).

The election was big news for anyone with a marketing idea and a decent connection to a Chinese factory. I was pondering Hope on a Rope myself, featuring forty-four's smiling face carved deep into a bar of soap. Who wouldn't pay $14.95 plus tax to shower with a president every morning? No? Well how about $4.95?

I still think it could work. As someone, I forget who, once said, you can't misunderestimate the American appetite for presidential paraphernalia.

Obama, who hasn't been able to quit smoking yet, shouldn't be surprised if people try to sell his butts on eBay.

And while we're on the subject, I wish everybody would leave him the hell alone about his occasional cigarette sneaking. If the leader of the free world wants to unwind with a cigarette after another day of listening to Republicans accuse him of everything short of bowling with the severed heads of their grandmothers, it's fine by me.

My sweet Lord, he's not firing up a crack pipe. I get that it's not good for him but I think Obama needs a few stress reducers. The man lives with his mother-in-law, for God's sake.

You think your boss is a jerk and your job at the widget factory is a stressful bummer? Try dealing on a daily basis with psychos like Kim Jong II and Congresswoman Michele Bachmann (R-Neptune). Not so easy now, is it?

It's not like he's grinding out the butts with his heel on the presidential seal of the Oval Office. Let him be. The man was awarded the Nobel Prize after approximately twenty seconds in office. Yes, yes, I know it's just because the Nobel folks hated Bush. They would've given it to *The Situation* if they could have gotten away with it.

Thanks to Obama's election, even the French are being nicer to Americans, although they still think we're too fat and spend way too much time carping about how much they smoke. In elementary school.

Obama never gets to truly relax. Not even at his own parties. Remember those goofballs who lied their way into the fancy state dinner for the prime minister of India?

What was the Secret Service doing? Talking into its shoe? Was it trapped in the Cone of Silence? What?

It's not Obama's fault that he was even photographed shaking hands with Tareq and Michaele Salahi. Everyone who's watched *The Princess Diaries* knows that the way this highfalutin political party stuff goes is that someone stands beside the fancy folks and whispers the names of the approaching guests. Unfortunately, the Salahis should've been introduced as "two assholes who have crashed your party by pretending to be on the list because they want to be on *Real Housewives of DC*, Mr. President. And, no, I'm not making this up."

So we now know that the Secret Service, for all its sexy

portrayal in the movies, basically has the technology of Laura Ingalls' chalk slate in *Little House on the Prairie*.

At a checkpoint, the Secret Service had a clipboard with the names of all the invited guests on it, but the gruesome twosome schmoozed their way in anyway.

A clipboard? Are you kidding me? This isn't the South Georgia debutante ball at the Ramada we're talking about. A clipboard? In this age of terrorism threats, the only thing we have in place to make sure POTUS isn't dusted with anthrax is the same thing they use for call-ahead seating at Red Lobster? Hell, even Costco demands a picture ID at the door.

Because I'm a political junkie from way back, I'm already looking ahead to 2012, when I'm hoping for a pop-culture dream ticket: Sarah Palin and La Toya Jackson.

Palin/Jackson is my fantasy ticket for the sheer hilarity of it. La Toya could point out perceived enemies ("Barney Frank murdered my brother!") and Say-ruh, as we say here in the South, could mow 'em down with her moose musket. ("I gotcher!")

Problem is, I'm not sure if La Toya Jackson is a Republican or a Democrat. My best guess is that she's a Martian. No matter. It's a simple change of registration.

Why Palin/Jackson? That's easy. These are power women who know how to generate a ton of ink. When people stopped talking about Palin after the 2008 election, she got right back in the spotlight for "ya know, doin' the quittin' thing because it's the ones who, ya know, stay in office and things like that, which erode our, ya know, values and stuff." And La Toya is fond of conspiracy theories which are, to borrow from the old *Addams Family* theme, "creepy and kooky, mysterious and spooky, altogether ooky."

Which is a great, underused word by the way.

La Toya Jackson on the ticket would accomplish the unimaginable: She would make Sarah Palin look like the sensible, articulate one. La Toya would be the wind beneath Palin's mounted bald eagle wings, as it were. Ooky.

La Toya would bring her own cabinet without even having to step out of the gene pool and put on a towel: Secretary of State Tito, Secretary of the Treasury Marlon, Secretary of Yo-Yo Dieting and Occasional Fitness Janet, and Secretary of All That Is Germane Jermaine.

And, yes, I know Say-ruh has smart-girl glasses and her caribou Manwiches are enough to make Greta Van Susteren swoon, but I'm not sure she's interesting enough by herself to be president. Which, make no mistake, is where she's headed.

It has been said that the only way Sarah Palin can triumph is if good people do nothing. OK, I'm paraphrasing there. But do we really want to see first dude Todd doing doughnuts in his snowmobile on the White House front lawn, crushin' his empties on his big, vacant noggin, and refusing to recycle?

OK, maybe that does sound kinda cool now that I think about it.

If Palin gets elected, we can expect more shenanigans on the order of the Republican National Committee's now-famous fund-raising appeal that suggested that Democrats wanted to overhaul health care to deny treatment to Republicans.

Well, that's just nuts!

But then these are the same people who like to spread the rumor that Obama wants to personally suffocate Palin's precious special-needs child in his sleep and he will pay ACORN workers to peddle "kill Grandpa" pills door-to-door like copies of *The Watchtower*.

Remember how the Republicans whined about the Dems vilifying Bush? Oh, it was so awful, so disrespectful, so un-American. But things are different with Obama in the big house. Now, to quote the always acerbic Bill Maher, the far right believes Obama is so core-evil that his favorite hobby is beating nuns to death with truckloads of dead puppies.

But back to this notion that Dems will play favorites at the doctor's office. Really? Is there anyone besides those frumpy, red-eyed wailing women who show up at town hall meetings with their hair combs and prairie skirts (surely, the sister-wives are back at the compound) who could honestly believe that?

Although I seldom agree with Republicans, I'd never withhold medical care based on our political differences.

I believe Republicans are absolutely entitled to any and all medical treatments that they need and desire. In due time.

Kidding! No one seriously believes that doctors are going to check voter registrations before treating patients, do they? That would be a violation of the Hippopotamus Oath. Which

I'm not sure they have in Kenya, our president's *true* birthplace according to the frumpsters.

How would it even work?

Doctor: "Hmmmm. Bill, I know you and I go back a really long way and that I delivered all five of your children but, well, goshdarnit, it says here on your chart that you voted for Nixon in '72 so it seems to me that your appendix is just going to have to explode while we leave you for dead. Nurse! Go out in the waiting room and see if any Democrats are waiting out there. And make sure they're getting the good magazines, too."

Waaaaaaaahhhh.

25

Animal Tales and One
Stupid Human Trick

Next time Bubba and Billy Bob go fishing, they might discover that the fish more or less moseys onto the hook, languishes on the line, and then passively lays there in the cooler smoothing its scales instead of flailing.

Why come?

Because scientists have just discovered that estrogen in the water is making fish, particularly large-mouthed bass in the South, a whole lot less aggressive. In other words: Our Southern fish are "gender confused." Is it something in the water? Mayhaps. Because, among other reasons, Bobbie Jean has decided to pitch her birth control pills into the commode and all that estrogen gets into our waterways.

Further study has determined that most of the afflicted Southern bass have both male and female sex characteristics, so it's understandable that they're confused. Most of the time they don't know whether to pound beers with the guys at Buffalo Wild Wings or check out the semiannual shoe sale at Dillard's.

The only good news to come from this is that it could result in a recall of that horrid wall plaque with the singing bass on it. You know the one. Instead of *Take Me to the River*, perhaps some lilting show tunes would be in order.

It can't just be about Bobbie Jean, though, because it's not happening in other parts of the country. In Alaska, for instance, fish are completely free of this intersex condition. Alaskan fish have no gender confusion, preferring lumberjack plaid for the boys and something slightly slutty from Forever 21 for the girls.

Scientists say that this gender bending may keep fish from reproducing because, with so many in sexual limbo, there's just no real push to procreate.

Oh, if only deer, squirrels, and Kardashians would acquire this particular affliction. I'm just kidding. I don't really have anything against deer. Or squirrels.

If you're anything like me (and God help you if you are), you're probably already wondering how this is going to impact . . . your Friday night at Red Lobster. What? You thought I was going to say the environment?

The good news is that intersex fish, while perhaps emotionally conflicted, are perfectly safe to eat, scientists say. The absolute worst thing that would happen is that, if you're a boy, your bidness will fall off. What? Is that a problem?

I grew up fishing for bass so this is bad news for me. The fun is in the fight! If the fish simply yawns in my direction and suggests a light breading of panko crumbs with a modest pinot on the side, there's no real sport in that.

Of course, this is serious environmental business and a few of you who care about this sort of thing passionately will probably argue that this could be the start of an ecological nightmare and they wish my business would fall off, too, for making light of it all.

While I'm plenty worried about the fish never getting their groove back, there's an even bigger ecological threat to my beloved Southland than gender-confused fish, and it's slithering its way up the coast from Florida. According to a report released by the U.S. Geological Survey (motto: "Beer Makes Us Awesome!"), Floridians, whom I previously regarded as a peaceful people, have been releasing killer snakes into the wild willy-nilly.

Snakes being snakes, they aren't happy to hang out in Florida and they're heading north, where it's not so humid and there are better drivers.

News reports make it sound as if they're slithering along I-95, perhaps getting "stuck on Stuckey's" along the way and snake-giggling at the billboards for South of the Border. Because snakes don't have a GPS or even MapQuest, I'm not sure how they know the route but I guess it's instinctual. Kind of the same way that we humans have instinct that tells us how to care for our newborns and, even more important, to never let the skinny bitch in the group pick the restaurant. Instinct is very powerful stuff and snakes are up to their slitty little eyes with it.

So what are we to do about all these snakes heading up the coast? Well, I could give you a long, fancy-pants National Public Radio-induced answer, but the short version is, "Bend over and kiss your ass good-bye."

No, seriously. That's all any of us can do.

There's no stopping this army of big snakes because, scientists say, they can produce *one hundred baby snake eggs at a time*. I will pause now for y'all to go throw up.

Florida, what did we do to deserve this?

Turns out that owning that cute little Burmese python outlived its fun factor once BP grew up and wound his way around the lanai. What to do? You take the former pet for a ride and dump him out. Done!

No! Not done! When asked by a reporter if there were actually, honestly, giant snakes in metropolitan areas like Miami, a scientist responded, and this is a di-rect quote, "Yes."

Dude. Let us down easy. You don't just tell somebody that giant pythons are slithering around South Beach. Sure, the vapid movie stars and reality TV stars who tend to lounge about down there probably just think of a boa constrictor as uber Spanx, but the rest of us have enough sense to be scared.

Scientists are, technically speaking, "completely freaked out in the head" about this march of the giant snakes northward, squeezing and/or consuming everything in their path.

One scientist said since the snake march began, he's had the chance to peer into the stomachs of literally hundreds of dead pythons (and you thought your job sucked) and found basically everything except a Barcalounger in there.

While plenty of the killer snakes have been dumped by bored owners who are, if you ask me, nuttier than squirrel shit to even own these varmints in the first place, others are the descendants of snakes that escaped from pet shops back in '92, when Hurricane Andrew came calling. Said one scientist, "They escaped and have been reproducing ever since." Snakes, like the technology-starved Duggars, have to find themselves something interesting to do, I guess.

Scientists say these *house-sized snakes* can climb trees and take out entire species of birds, "akin to the situation with brown tree snakes on Guam."

Oh, holy Lord! Not the brown tree snakes of Guam! Wait a minute. What?

Scientists say the giant Burmese python in particular could be heading north. I looked up the giant Burmese python because knowledge, along with a working shotgun, is power. Turns out its favorite hobbies are "eating everything in its path, reproducing with abandon, and traveling long distances." Sounds like all of my old boyfriends once they dumped me.

Maybe I shouldn't be so paranoid about snakes, or so worried about the fish population. The human animal is the one we should all worry about the most because it's the stupidest.

A quick illustration: Redneck cousins Joe and Jacky Ray were out hunting big snakes one day when they happened upon a huge hole in the ground.

The closer they got to the hole, the more they were amazed by the sheer size of it. Like any good rednecks, they immediately decided that the best idea in the world would be to figure out exactly how deep it was.

"Let's chunk something down in there," said Jacky Ray, the brains of the two. "We could throw it down and then listen hard to see how long it takes to hit the bottom."

Joe thought this was a pretty great idea because, yes, he did just eat a bowl of stupid for breakfast.

Jacky Ray glanced over behind him and saw a rusty old car transmission sitting off to the side.

"Gimme a hand," he said to Joe. "We'll take this here transmission and throw it in that hole and see how long it takes 'fore it hits bottom."

So the two of 'em picked up the transmission and hauled it over to the big hole. They counted one-two-three and heaved the transmission into the hole, then stood close to the edge listening for it to hit bottom. All of a sudden, they heard a rustling sound in the brush behind them. Jacky Ray and Joe turned around and saw a wild-eyed goat come crashing through the brush, run up to the hole and, with not so much as a second's hesitation, jump into that big hole, headfirst.

Jacky Ray and Joe had never seen anything like this kind of animal behavior so they just stood there, slack jawed, looking at each other and looking back into the hole, trying to figure out what the hell just happened.

An old farmer walked up right about then and asked them, "You fellows didn't happen to see my goat around here anywhere, did you?"

And Joe said, "Well, that's funny you should ask that, mister. We were just standing here a minute ago and a goat came running out of the bushes doin' I'd say a hunncrt miles an hour and just jumped headfirst into this hole here!"

The old farmer shook his head and said, "Why that's impossible. I had him chained to a transmission."

26

Lost in Space

While it's awfully tempting to sneer at girl-astronaut Heidemarie Stefanyshyn-Piper for losing a $100,000 tool kit during a space walk, I just say: You. Go. Girl.

It was brilliant really. There's poor HSP working with a (ick!) grease gun and, while she's cleaning up, the bag "slips" out of her grip, the tools tumble into the final frontier, and back at NASA Mission Control, they hear her mumble, "Oh, great."

Yes, great! Great way to make sure that from now on, maybe they'll let you stay inside the cute capsule thingy and make muffins for the rest of the crew. Crazy like a fox, you!

I'm only slightly worried that one day in the next few years, some poor kid growing up in an Oklahoma trailer park is going to get hit in the head by that thing falling from outer space.

"Son, I bet that's the grease gun that girl astronaut lost a few years back," his daddy will say. "Whoa. That's gonna leave a mark."

I decided HSP did it on purpose to get out of work because, like I said, she wasn't nearly as contrite as she should've been after losing the expensive tools used to maintain the spacecraft. Her explanation:

"Despite my little hiccup, I think we did a great job out there!"

This would appear to be a slammin' new version of the old chestnut, "But other than that, Mrs. Lincoln, how did you like the play?" A little hiccup?

NASA, once again finding itself with powdered egg in a tube on its collective face, didn't have the reaction I would've predicted.

I was expecting NASA to issue a stern rebuke of such carelessness. Perhaps even something along the lines of "Are you a freakin' moron? It's not like y'all can head on over to Home Depot and pick up some new tools? That bastard costs *one hundred thousand dollars!*"

But, no. NASA took a kinder, gentler approach with the loss of the taxpayer-funded tool bag, issuing a statement praising HSP and saying, "she showed real character and great discipline" by continuing on and doing a fine job for the rest of the spacewalk. Not to belabor the point, but where did they think she could've gone? *She's in space.* It's not like she can say, "Screw all of y'all, there's a sale at Pier 1 and I am *so* outta here, asshats. Uhhhh. Which way was Earth again?"

Because NASA isn't completely stupid and apparently never misses a BOGO on tool bags, our girl was told that she could continue her chore by sharing her fellow astronaut's tool bag, which I'm sure pleased him no end. ("You think you can hold onto that caulking gun? It belonged to my grand-daddy. . . .")

NASA did say it was a trifle odd that she "lost" the tool kit because normally it's tethered to a much larger bag. Maybe she just thought they didn't go together. Tandem bags are just so 1998, y'all.

The spin doctors at Mission Control managed to make it seem almost laudable that there's a bag of expensive-ass space-ship parts floating out there.

"We appreciate how hard you all are working," they said in a peppy little post-goof message to the crew. Which makes me just wonder if NASA is, well, high.

The next goal for the space team is to build a $154 million machine that will convert urine to drinking water. Which means HSP's muffins may taste kinda funny, at least on the first couple of tries. It's like when you make pancakes and you always have to throw out the first two or three 'cause the griddle isn't hot enough yet and you've used too much urine, er, water.

Why am I so cranky about my astro-sistah? Because she sets us all backward when she does dumb shit like that. She, of all people, should know that women still have to work twice as hard in male-dominated professions just to be taken seriously. That's not fair, of course, but it's true. So when you, oopsie, lose a tool kit, it causes heartless humor writers everywhere to unveil snarky, personal attacks on all of womankind. Thank God she didn't whine that the orange spacesuit didn't do a thing for her complexion.

To be fair (which, incidentally, I just hate) HSP has been a good, occasionally outstanding, astronaut for more than a decade, so that does make me think the whole losing-the-tool-kit thing was planned. I mean, it did happen while she was *cleaning up* a greasy mess. Maybe she got fed up with always being the one who had to clean up the guys' mess. Maybe she was all "Right stuff, *this*, bitches!" Or, maybe not.

In any case, it's important to remember that anybody can make a mistake, especially when you're the only girl living with a bunch of men whose only core belief is that bacon makes everything better. Stuck in space without so much as a *Jersey Shore* rerun, their main job was to add a couple of rooms to your "house." Only in this case, the house is a space station, and they're transforming it to a five-bedroom, two-bath home with a kitchen.

I imagine astrogirl may have grown a little tired of being surrounded by all that testosterone. If you've ever experienced a major renovation project with a member of the opposite sex, you understand that tensions can run high.

I bet they hooted her down when she wanted to talk paint chips and fabric swatches.

Yes, the more I think about it, it's entirely likely that I'm being way too hard on HSP. I can't say that I could've survived more than a single day living with a bunch of guys, wearing that unflattering-ass color, and knowing that when they did finally get that urine-to-water gizmo hooked up and working right, they'd just nag her to try to figure out a way to turn urine into beer.

Things haven't been easy for NASA lately. The moon program had such a bad case of been-there-done-that that its funding's been killed. But, no matter, they're rebounding with a plan to work with private companies to develop space taxis. In theory, this sounds pretty cool, but then you have to think how sometimes it's hard to even get a cab across town.

The plan is for NASA to pay private space taxis to take their astronauts up to the space station for about $20 million per passenger. So I guess the astronauts will need to stand out on the curb holding up giant pillowcases with dollar signs on them to get the attention of the cabbie.

Of course, regular folks can pay for a ride, too, using these space taxis that, with any luck at all, will be operated by drivers who won't be talking on their damn cell phones the entire time. Which wouldn't be bad, because I love to eavesdrop, if they didn't mumble so much that the only thing you can hear is, like, every tenth word, which sometimes sounds like ". . . terrorist . . . explosion . . . jihad . . . meatless patties . . ."—all of which are equally scary in my paranoid brain.

At the end of the trip to the space station, will the space taxi driver press that little button on the right and make the fare miraculously jump by 20 percent for *no apparent reason?* Will he then explain that it's because of some bullshit "time-of-day surcharge"? Will you then get all pissy and make him take you back to Earth so you can go to an ATM and withdraw enough cash to pay his greedy butt?

And wouldn't it be fun if these new space taxis would occasionally have a *Cash Cab* driver? (On second thought, *Cash Cab* wouldn't be a great fit because if you fail to answer all the questions right on the show, you're ejected without prize money. It would be hard to pull over near what used to be Pluto and dump the riders just because they didn't know the capital of North Dakota.)

Interestingly, one of the major backers of the new space taxi business is the founder of Amazon.

And because of this, I worry that if duh-hubby and I buy our space taxi tickets one day, he'll go first in a separate "shipment" for no apparent reason while I may arrive, inexplicably, days to weeks later.

Another space taxi playa is the founder of a California company that has already built a rocket called Falcon and a capsule called Dragon. Which reminds me, his mommy said it was time for his lunch and not to forget to drink all his milk.

NASA says that in the future, there will be multiple spaceships carrying crews, pushing costs down and safety up. Hmmm. Perhaps they will follow the successful route of traditional airline transportation. Only this way, instead of paying $99 for your one-way flight to Albuquerque and getting your flight canceled or delayed so you can spend more time perusing the offerings at Jamba Juice and watching the hair grow on your legs, you will be able to pay $20 million to be bumped or otherwise inconvenienced.

Once you finally board your space taxi, because it's a taxi, I'm guessing the food offerings will be more in keeping with that kind of ambiance, say a bag of Funyuns and some formerly urine turned water.

Of course, this is many years away, partly because the technology isn't completely in place and there are still many seed grants to divvy up between competing companies. Not only that, it's going to take a long time to round up a sufficient number of religious icons to place on the dashboard.

Y'all know I'm right.

27

She Drives Me Crazy
(Shaving Time Off the Commute)

My friend Randy is 'bout to lose his religion over his new car.

A good Southern boy, Randy was tickled with his car at first because it (a) has plenty of leg room (b) dual sunroofs and (c) isn't a Toyota.

Randy's car is awesome in many regards but it was the state-of-the-art navigation system that sold him.

Who that, you ask? Well, it's a fab little device that lets you keep your eye on the road while you "talk" to your car. Randy likes to use the system to call people, hands free, or, more often, to command it to play music.

Unfortunately, his car can't understand Randy's melodious Southern drawl.

"I don't know what I'm gonna do," Randy told me. "I tell

it, as plain as I know how, to 'Play artist Hall and Oates' and it will come back with this hateful Yankee voice that snaps at me, 'I didn't understand you.' So then I say, 'I said Hall and Oates, *por favor*' because I'm feeling just a little bit hateful and I might as *well* be speaking in a furrin language.

"So I say again to the machine, 'Play *Rich Girl*.' It's one of my favorites. I remember the first time I heard it I was in high school and it had been out for a long time but I really liked it because I was actually dating a kinda rich girl at the time and what *was* her name? . . . She was really cute but a little taller than my usual girlfriends, 'cause you know I'm cursed in the height department. All the Wagram men are. My Uncle Elvin was short, but he never had any trouble with the women. He liked 'em young with old money. I'll never forget when his mama, who was a real piece of work, got introduced to his newest woman friend and she was way different from his usual teenyboppers. She must've been at least forty-five which was perfect because Elvin was close to fifty. Anyway, Aunt Berle had been sipping cocktails for a couple of hours, and when he introduced his new grown-up woman friend to Berle and explained how she owned a highly successful chain of lawn furniture stores, Aunt Berle said, 'Well how 'bout that! Usually Elvin goes for young poontang and old money, not old poontang and new money. That boy's just full of surprises, I reckon.' Anywho, I loved that song *Rich Girl* and had just developed a real hankerin' to hear it and so I was talking about old times and *that Yankee bitch just cut me off!*"

Well, as a typical Southerner, Randy may go on just a bit. And it's possible that he even forgot for a second that he was talking to a machine. You know those people that you describe as "he never met a stranger"? That's Randy. Except sometimes I want to say a stranger what.

Randy says that his car's navigation system's inability to understand his Southern accent means that he arrives everywhere just a little pissed off.

"That crazy Yankee bitch inside my car hears Derek and the Dominos as Death Cab for Cutie," he said morosely. "I haven't been this upset since they put me on the prayer chain at church for foot fungus. You know, I just hate when everybody has to know my business. That prayer chain is something to be scared of. The Baptists print the reason for the prayers right there in the bulletin, you know, so I was embarrassed to wear sandals for a very long time."

Oh, yes, well . . .

Randy says he gets so upset sometimes that he just pulls over to the shoulder of the interstate and takes a few minutes to cuss out his car.

I told Randy that I was completely sympathetic. And as a member of the pseudojournalistic profession, I plan to investigate this thoroughly and get back to him with the results of my in-depth research and extensive interviews.

Kidding! I haven't got time for that shit. But I do get it. I told Randy that I have the same problem every time I "tawk" to a phone tree.

I don't think I've ever used directory assistance without a real human having to come on the line to figure out what the hell I'm trying to say.

The computer says, "What listing?" in that clipped tone that indicates you better get it right the first time.

So I say something perfectly normal, taking care to enunciate perfectly: "Ah'd lock da numbah for Bream Baituh's Worms and Cawfee Shop, puleeeeez," which any moron should be able to understand, but no!

This is followed by that hateful pause and "Please hold for an operator."

Randy will, I'm afraid, just have to get used to the fact that the rest of the country tawks funny. They can't hep theyselves.

He shouldn't oughta be talking on the phone while driving anyway. Even hands-free devices aren't safe.

You know what's even less safe than talking on the phone or even texting or reading the newspaper while driving? Shaving your cootch, that's what.

Well. You asked.

Florida driver Megan Barnes wins the Lifetime Redneck Achievement Award for her behavior while driving along the Keys on a balmy March day.

Megan decided to multitask, as we all have at one time or another, while she was enroute to a date. But while we've all done dumb things like applying eye shadow or mascara at the stop light when we're running short of time, Megan took the whole grooming-while-driving to new heights. That's right: She decided that she'd use the drive time to spruce up her love rug.

Unfortunately for Megan, this required more attention than she could safely give such an intimate project so, mid-shave, she slammed into the back of a pickup truck at forty-five miles per hour.

That kinda makes the time you drove with your elbows while eating a Whopper seem downright virtuous, doesn't it?

I'm trying to remember back to my driver's education classes, and I swear I don't remember Mr. Kilpatrick ever coming right out and saying, "Whatever you do, young ladies, do not ever be tempted to trim your hoohah while you're behind the wheel." No, I would've definitely remembered that, and I'm certain there was no grisly video to watch that showed such behavior.

Ms. Barnes told the investigating officer that she was "on her way to a date and wanted to be ready for the visit."

Yes, she wanted to look her best. All over. Except, well, I've seen Ms. Barnes' mug shot and she has a face that would stop a clock and raise hell with small watches. I don't want to sound cruel, but you'd have to be pretty walleyed to even make it as far as her hoohah, bless her heart.

I guess the only thing to be grateful for in this sorry scenario is that Ms. Barnes didn't try to *wax* her bidness while driving. Imagine the horror if she'd tossed the used wax strips into the waterway as she cruised toward Key West.

Talk about saving the manatees. They might've thought those were the pelts of long-lost cousins.

I've driven this particular stretch of highway a few times in my life and it's one of the prettiest drives imaginable: crystal waters, cloudless skies, gorgeous mangroves. Call me crazy but I've never been so bored that I decided to drag a sharp blade over my naughties just to have something to do.

In all fairness, Ms. Barnes was smart enough to realize that she couldn't shave and steer simultaneously so she asked the passenger in the front seat, who happened to be her *ex husband*, to take the wheel while she got busy. What a guy! How many men do you know who would help their ex get ready for a big date in quite this manner?

And how did that conversation go, you reckon?

"Here, hon, hold the wheel for a few minutes. I'm gonna hook up with Ray-Ray when we hit Long Key and I wanna try to make it look like a *lightning bolt!*"

Precious Lord.

Not only did Ms. Barnes' ex agree to take the wheel, but after the wreck, he switched places and tried to take the blame, too.

Unfortunately, his bare chest sold him out. The airbag only deployed on the passenger side and our white knight (OK, actually more of a pawn) had the bruises to prove it.

To nobody's real surprise, the Florida Highway Patrol quickly discovered that Ms. Barnes didn't have a valid driver's license. Oh, and the day before, she'd been convicted of

DUI. (Everybody say, "Noooooooo!!!!!") Oh, and her car had been seized and had no insurance or registration. (It was a Thunderbird, if you were wondering. Yes, she was having fun, fun, fun' til the po-lice took her T-bird awaaaaayyy.) Oh, and she was a probationer. Albeit an impeccably groomed one.

I imagine that Megan Barnes' tale will be legendary in the Keys and beyond for many years to come. And, thanks to her foolishness, there will doubtless be a new warning label on your razors and shaving products. Because every time a dumb ass does something like this, the companies involved feel the need to explain the dangers to prevent possible lawsuits.

Something along the lines of "Warning! Do not attempt to use this razor in the vicinity of your cooter while driving. Failure to use this product in the safety and sanctity of your bathroom will result in unremitting grossness and possible harm to yourself and others."

Because these warnings must be accompanied by simple drawings that transcend language barriers, it should be one hell of a picture, am I right?

I told this story to Randy to get his mind off his own language problems, but it didn't help all that much. He's decided to accept his Aunt Berle's wisdom on such matters.

"She always says that which does not kill us only makes us meaner."

She's a feisty one, that Berle.

28

Teen Angel

While observing, Margaret Mead-style, the behaviors of the older siblings of Sophie's friends, I realized they didn't have any idea that, to me, they were simply Aéropostale-clothed canaries in the puberty coal mine—fluttering, daffy, and occasionally mean-as-hell canaries that would reveal the future of drama to come.

And now it's here.

Not in a bad way, mostly, maybe just a four on the scale of one to "*OMG, you are such a creeper!*" shouted at some kid whose only crime was to sit just a little too close on the activity bus. At this tender age, everything is a tad ramped up, hyped, jazzed, and a few other moldy expressions from many decades ago.

Hormones are kicking in around here. What an odd twist

of nature that the Princess should be entering this phase of her life at the precise moment that I'm leaving it and pondering the indignity of chin tweezing.

But this is as it should be, and I'm not so old that I don't recall, painfully well, what it was like to be thirteen.

The thing that has puzzled Duh and me in this new phase, as we watch the Princess navigate these never-still waters, is how fickle and fast-moving the relationships are between girl and girl and boy and girl. We have actually dropped her off at the movies with her friends only to hear that, by the time we pick them up, one boy in the group has texted another girl, the girl has responded, and now the original couple has "broken up" after being together, all in less than three hours.

Me: "Why is Paul walking with Sarah when his movie date was Katie?"

Princess: "Ohmigod, that was *hours* ago. Paul said that he and Katie are going to just be friends."

Me: "But they were boyfriend/girlfriend just three hours ago. What could've possibly changed?"

Princess: "Well, Katie said that Paul was emotionally unavailable while they were getting popcorn and she just doesn't think that she can put up with all the drama."

Me: "What drama? The guy just wants to decide what flavor of frozen Coke he gets."

Princess: "Yeah, but they kinda like other people, anyway."

Me: "They found this out in the time it took to get their snacks and the opening credits to roll?"

Princess: (bored with this) "What? Yeah, I guess so. There's no point in wasting time on a relationship when you know it's not going to go anywhere."

Me: *"But it was only sixteen minutes!"*

Part of me admires the brisk "cut your losses" mentality of the teen generation but, if this keeps up, marriage vows are going to be hugely problematic.

Minister: ". . . to have and to hold from this day forward. . . ."

Couple (in unison): "Uhhhhhhhh . . . about that. . . ."

The phrase "going out" is eternally comical to us, which only irritates the Princess even more.

Princess: "Claire and Michael are going out! They are, like, perfect for each other. They are, like, the . . . best . . . couple . . . ever."

Me: "What do you mean, going out? We used to call it going together or going steady."

Princess: "Same thing, but we call it going out."

Me: "But they don't really go anywhere, do they? You said they were going out, but they've only just talked at school or on the phone, right? That hardly constitutes going out."

Princess: (*Deep, impatient sigh*): "It doesn't mean they're going out somewhere. God! Do you always have to *make fun of the way I talk?*"

Me: "Well, I was just trying to understand."

Princess: "Look, they're going out. And they'll be together tonight when we go to the movies, a bunch of us, if you'll drive us and give me twenty dollars for popcorn 'cause I need to buy some candy for Sophia to pay her back because she loaned me some money last time and she was, like, it's really OK, I don't mind lending it to you and I was, like, well, I hate to take your money because it's really not, like, I have to have Gobstoppers but then she was, like, Oh, no, you have to take it, and I was like . . ."

Me: (*looking at grocery flier*) "Yay! There's a BOGO on non-dairy creamer this week!"

Princess:

Me: "OK, well, sure, if you owe someone money, you need to pay them back, but you should earn the money from doing chores around the house."

Princess: "*It's always all about the money! Oh my God!*"

Me: "OK, honey, let's ratchet it down a few thousand notches, shall we? Go sweep the patio and you can earn some money toward the movie ticket."

Princess:

Me: "Or you can stay home with Daddy and me and we'll watch the *Andy Griffith Show* marathon and pop some corn. It'll be just as much fun as being with your friends!"

Princess: "But I *have* to go! Everyone else is going! I will physically *die* if I don't go!"

Uh-huh. Although I know I'm right about this, it's not productive to point out that no one has ever died from *not* seeing a Johnny Depp movie on the night it opens.

After earning the movie money, there will much angst about What to Wear. Clothes will be pulled off hangers and out of drawers and heaped onto bed and floor before the inevitable wailing.

"I have no clothes," she will say quietly and simply. "None at all. Not. One. Thing."

At this point, I've learned it's not a great idea to point out that, through different combinations and pairings, there are, mathematically speaking, at least 422 possible outfits littering her room, which now looks as though Anthropologie has had a terrible stomach ache and thrown up all over everything.

Cautiously, I pick up a pair of jeans and a cute top from Urban Outfitters. "What about this?"

The Princess gasps. "Oh! I didn't even *see* that. Thanks, Mommie!"

Logic has no place in these occasional thunderstorm conversations which, as quickly as they arrive, drift out on a Clearasil sea, and she returns, rather like the adorable Regan in *The Exorcist* after an "episode," with childlike playfulness and affection. Nope, I'm not going to have to summon two priests to the house. Yet.

I feel a little sorry for Duh because he is trapped between two females, both affected by occasional swings of hormonal havoc, and there's really nothing he can do except excuse himself to go "oil the lawnmower," which is unnecessary in January and smacks of snipe-hunting, if you ask me.

The boy/girl stuff is comical but the girl/girl stuff? Not so much. As any parent of a middle-school girl knows, it's possible to be "besties" and "BFFs" with a girl on Wednesday and mortal enemies with her by Friday.

Happens all the time.

In fact, everything happens so much faster now because friends are recruited, courted, and dropped via text or Facebook in a matter of minutes.

I refrain from telling the Princess how it was back in the day when we simply relied on passed notes, which seldom made it to their destination but almost always ended up in the teacher's hands. She would sigh at the note's contents, look heavenward and tear it into confetti. No box would be checked "yes" or "no" on matters of utmost importance.

It hurts to be dropped by a friend, and hurts exponentially to be dropped by a pack of 'em. You don't ever really forget that and, if it happens, it's important to take inspiration from whatever role model can offer the most wisdom. In my case, it was a certain prom queen named Carrie.

In the Princess' "posse," there is constant drama, most of it exceedingly silly and, mercifully, patched up by the end of the day. In the meantime, however, there can be tears and recriminations worthy of a Telemundo soap opera.

Verdad that.

Although the technology makes everything faster and more poorly spelled, nothing is really all that different than when I was thirteen.

"Ayden didn't sit with me at lunch because she said that she heard that I said that she was sexting some eighth-grade guy that I don't even know," said a despondent Princess one day.

Sexting? *sexting???????*

I told myself to breathe deeply. What would Carrie do? No, I mean what would a rational, calm super parent do? Who can I channel for something this important? Who????"

Because I get most of my mad parenting skills from watching TV, I decided to use a multifaceted approach from some of the characters we've already discussed here.

Kate Gosselin: "Sexting? I believe I need this boy's name and his parents' phone number and I need it yesterday. Do I think he'd be willing to go on my talk show? Yes, I do. I hope so, anyway. It's sweeps month and I need something besides complaining about how much I hate media attention. Somebody call my publicist."

Oprah: "Sexting? Is that like the time Stedman emailed me to ask what I was wearing? Of course it turned out that was just so we wouldn't clash on the red carpet. . . ."

Dr. Phil: "Sexting? How's that workin' for you? Huh? I don't know, I just like asking that. I'm pretty much a doofus. Tennis?"

Betty Draper: "Sexting? Young lady, bring me the Lifebuoy this minute. Good. Now open your mouth and do not move until your father comes home. A week from Thursday."

The Neelys: "Sexting? Mmmmm. That sounds naisty! We're in!"

My go-to cast of characters was clearly not going to be any help. So I sat down and talked. I talked for a very long time, lovingly and calmly, about all the perils out there and how it will take a strong moral core to deal with them. Throughout, the Princess smiled and nodded and seemed to be taking it all in. Yes, I was parent of the year, brimming with warmth and wisdom.

And then, she flipped back her hair and I saw the little earbuds. She had been listening to her iPod the whole time!

Utterly defeated, I motioned to her to take out her earbuds.

"Did you hear anything I said?" I asked her, feeling incredibly foolish.

"Hmmm?" she asked, giving me an odd little grin. "Not a word." I turned to leave and got all the way to the door before I heard her say, very softly, "And thanks."

Acknowledgments

Every encouraging word, shared memory, and funny story has powered me up and onward and I am truly grateful to a slew of wonderful folks for sustaining and inspiring me in more ways than I can count. They include: Luleen Anderson, Bob Bauman, Leon Brown, Lucy Bell, Nathan Bell, Diane Minshew, Debbie Houlditch, Beth Blackwell, Joe and Mary Ellen Bonczyk (the perfect couple, for real), Todd Depriest, John Bell, Rachel Jones, Mary Seelye, David and Renee Zukerman, Kara Chiles Sirmans, "Cracker Queen" Lauretta Hannon, Susan Reinhardt, Kathy Patrick, Ronda Rich, Jill Conner Browne, Jim and Rhonda Desmond, Danna Moles, Deborah Goodman, the incomparable Gina White Francis, David and Julie Fredericksen, Wayne Jackson, Lynn Manock, Brenda Hankins, "positive, encouraging" Kelly Jefferson, E.T. Rooks,

Acknowledgments

David Willard, David High, Martha Raynor, Jim and Denise Jones, Leila Viteskic, Neil Purdy, Pam Reade, Nancy Smith, Frank Stasio, Kinah Lindsey, Jo Tilghman, Brooks Preik, Angela Carr, Wanda Jewell, Nicki Leone, Cathy Stanley, Nancy Olson, Rene Martin, Ben Steelman, John Staton, Jeff Hidek, Cheryl Whitaker, Barb Ellis, Betty Ann Sanders, Randy ("Mr. Southport") Jones, Shirley and Woody Wilson, Linda Lavin, Wayne Jackson, Beth Perry, Hilarie Burton, Linda Patton, Kathleen Jewel, Ken Wells, Brad White, Verna Jordan, Keri Hooks, Bill Bartow, Catherine Perry, Elizabeth Redenbaugh, Shelly Hobson, Julia and Kelly Jewell, Laura Mitchell, Jim and Jeannie Skane, Tim and Pam Russell, Gray Wells, Pam Sander, Angela Stilley, Page Rutledge, Fran Mehurg, Tish Baker, Dana Sachs, Lisa and Mike Seifert, Teresa Hill, the fabulous twin muses of Lisa Noecker and Amy Mackay, Jemila Erickson, Nan Graham, the entire staff of public radio station WHQR-FM, Jana Moore, Debbi Pratt, Michelle Powell, Susan Pleasants, Burke Speaker, Banyan Restaurant, Jean Lee and Shirley, Jim Walker, Karel Dutton, Nancy Smith, Gary, Renee and Madison Barrett, Nancy Hosea, Bess Shadrach, the Halterman Family, Clyde Edgerton, Jill McCorkle, Laurie Notaro, Haven Kimmel, Hollis Gillispie, John Boy and Billy, Lee Smith, P.D. and Carol Midgette, Jimmy Bowden, Trey Wyatt, the 2009 UNC Men's Basketball Team, Caroline Rivenbark, Nancy Whisnant, and all the assorted Rivenbarks and Whisnants, St. Martin's Press's amazing Jennifer Enderlin, John Karle, Sara

Acknowledgments

Goodman, and Monica Katz, and "Tenacious J.," Jenny Bent of The Bent Agency.

Every single one of you has, as the kids say, "done me a solid" (some have done many, many solids) at some time in your life and I want you to know how much I appreciate it. A few of you may not even remember it, but I do. And I'm grateful.

To my husband, Scott Whisnant, let me just say that I'd let fake Vegas Elvis marry us again every day for eternity because you are that awesome. And also because I really like hearing him sing. And to my precious Princess, Sophie Caroline Whisnant, darling, if you read this, try to ignore all the cuss words. Mommie feels marginally nervous and guilty about them, although you'd never be able to tell. Because, as you know, I don't sweat much for a fat girl.

Celia Rivenbark
Wilmington, North Carolina